My Best Friend's
Birthday

The Making of a Quentin Tarantino Film

by
Andrew J. Rausch

**My Best Friend's Birthday:
The Making of a Quentin Tarantino Film**
©2019 Andrew J. Rausch

All rights reserved.

All photographs credited to Todd Henschell were taken by and are copywritten by Todd Henschell. They appear by permission of Todd Henschell.

No part of this book may be reproduced in any form or by any means, electronic, mechanical, digital, photocopying, or recording, except for inclusion of a review, without permission in writing from the publisher.

Published in the USA by:

BearManor Media
4700 Millenia Blvd.
Suite 175 PMB 90497
Orlando, FL 32839
www.BearManorMedia.com

ISBN: 978-1-62933-483-7 (alk. paper)

Design and Layout: Valerie Thompson

It was a lovely time in my life. It was my film school.
— QUENTIN TARANTINO

It's a real diamond in the rough. You can see Quentin's style starting to form, the beginnings are there... We didn't really know what we were doing at the time. The fun thing about it is we threw caution to the wind and just decided to make a movie. Quentin's genius was obvious even back then; he was extraordinary. He took what should have been a bad student film and ended up with a French farce, or a very funny film noir.
— CRAIG HAMANN

Had we ever finished the film it would have looked something like a sloppy version of She's Gotta Have It; *a miracle considering the budget.*
— ROGER AVARY

Dedicated to the memory of
JAMES BEST
AL HARRELL
DENNIS HUMBERT
CATHRYN JAYMES
SCOTT MCGILL
STEVO POLYI

FILM CAST

Craig Hamann as Mickey Burnett
Quentin Tarantino as Clarence Pool
Crystal Shaw Martell as Misty
Allen Garfield as Bill Smith
Al Harrell as Clifford
Brenda Hillhouse as Mrs. Smith
Linda Kaye as Pandora
Stevo Polyi as Clancy
Alan Sanborn as Nutmeg
Rich Turner as Oliver Brandon
Ronald Coleman as Ronny
Rowland Wafford as Lenny Otis
Leeane Chambers as Cecilia
David O'Hara as Eddie

FILM CREW

Quentin Tarantino, co-writer, director, producer, editor
Craig Hamann, co-writer, producer
Roger Avary, producer
Rand Vossler, cinematographer
Scott McGill, cinematographer
Roberto A. Quezada, cinematographer
Dov Schwarz, sound
Alan Sanborn, production assistant
Simon Ouwerkerk, technician

Norman Ouwerkerk, technician
Mike Davis, technician
Fred Olen Ray, camera provider
Todd Henschell, set photographer

TABLE OF CONTENTS

Notes and Acknowledgments . . . **1**

Foreword: The Significance of *My Best Friend's Birthday* . . . **3**

The *Shock Cinema* "Rosetta Stone" Review
   by Steven Puchalski . . . **9**

PART ONE

Introduction: Be Your Own Film School by Kieran Fisher . . . **13**

The Pieces Come Together . . . **17**

PART TWO

Introduction: This Is My On-Set Story, Tell Me Yours
   by Jason Pankoke . . . **65**

Making Movies . . . **69**

PART THREE

Introduction: Do You See the Same Cake?
   by Stephen Spignesi . . . **155**

Script and Film Breakdown . . . **159**

NOTES AND ACKNOWLEDGMENTS

The following people were interviewed by the author: Roger Avary, Jami Bernard, Craig Hamann, Todd Henschell, Brenda Hillhouse, Dennis Humbert, Linda Kaye, Jack Lucarelli, Crystal Shaw Martell, Steve Martinez, Don Murphy, David O'Hara, Fred Olen Ray, Alan Sanborn, Richard Squeri, Quentin Tarantino, Rand Vossler, Russell Vossler, Jeannie Wilson, and Connie Zastoupil. (It should be noted that some interviews were conducted by the author previously for other projects and were not done expressly for this book.)

The author would like to formally apologize to Linda Kaye for losing her prized photograph of the actress with Tarantino and Bruce Willis. ("She *should* be mad at you!" joked Tarantino. And he's right. Unfortunately, he said he didn't have "any spare photos" of himself with Linda and Bruce lying around, so he couldn't help.) It was an honest mistake and I'm truly sorry for losing this cherished and irreplaceable memento. I didn't realize it was the original copy.

The author would like to thank Tarantino's faithful assistant, Mayra Garcia, who was a tremendous help on this project. After Tarantino and I kept missing one another, Mayra worked hard to make sure Tarantino's involvement in the project happened.

FOREWORD: THE SIGNIFICANCE OF *MY BEST FRIEND'S BIRTHDAY*

I've admired Quentin Tarantino's work since I first discovered it on opening night of *Pulp Fiction* in 1994. (He's one hundred percent the reason I write crime fiction today. I also credit Elmore Leonard, but the truth is I only discovered Leonard through Tarantino. To call Tarantino an influence would be as big an understatement as saying Jesus was one of the people in the Bible.)

The man is a genius. His critics attempt to discount his work by saying his films are nothing more than pastiches of preexisting works, but there is more than that. These people don't understand art or the process of storytelling. Tarantino famously said, "Great artists steal." While this is accurate, it's so ridiculously oversimplified that he, in much the same way Stephen King did when he proclaimed himself the "literary equivalent of a Big Mac," did himself a tremendous disservice, providing ammunition to naysayers and dramatically understating his own merit.

Great artists lift ideas from other works, but in truth this isn't stealing as much as reworking and re-appropriating familiar themes and scenarios. Great artists don't lift every aspect of their work, but they do borrow elements. All of them. Every single one. There's an old adage that there's nothing new under the sun, and this is accurate. Need an example? I'll give you plenty. Let's look at a few modern classics: *The Shape of Water, No Country for Old Men, Chicago, The Shawshank Redemption,* and *Avatar*. All of these films are original, but all owe a significant debt to previously existing works. Can you deny that *The Shape of Water* is an aquatic re-imagining of *Beauty and the Beast*? *No Country for Old Men* isn't wholly original, either. Stories of cops tracking deadly killers are nothing new. These types of stories have been around forever; *Badlands* and *A Perfect World* are examples. In fact, the Tarantino-originated *Natural Born Killers* treads many of these same paths. It cannot be denied there are significant elements of *Silence of the Lambs* in *No Country*, as well.

Chicago is exactly like every single 1930s gangster film ever, only with the addition of singing and dancing (if we can call what Richard Gere does "singing"). *The Shawshank Redemption* is similar to every prison break movie ever, and additionally, its idea of a prisoner caring for a baby bird is directly lifted from the prison escape movie *The Birdman of Alcatraz*. (*Shawshank* author Stephen King later used this concept again, transforming the bird into a mouse in *The Green Mile*.) And *Avatar*... *Avatar* is *Pocahontas* with blue people. But these works are still valid, and they're still exceptional works of art. Yes, they reuse ideas and concepts from preexisting works, but they update them and put unique spins on them. This is what Quentin Tarantino does. And each time he lifts something, he dramatically improves it.

This is nothing new. *Star Wars* is a science fiction reworking of Akira Kurosawa's *The Hidden Fortress*, just as *Enemy Mine* is a sci-fi retelling of *Hell in the Pacific*. *Cujo* is *Jaws* on land. Every single slasher movie ever owes a tremendous debt to *Psycho*. John Carpenter's *Assault on Precinct 13* is a blatant reworking of *Rio Bravo* set in a jailhouse. Every single zombie movie depicting zombies eating human flesh is a reworking of *Night of the Living Dead*. Nearly every work of fiction (no matter the medium) contains elements of preexisting works.

But enough of that. Quentin Tarantino is an artist in every way. Whether or not you believe that does not change its being true. There's a reason he's been nominated for the Best Screenplay Oscar three times (winning twice) and Best Director twice. He's received tons of accolades, three of his films have been nominated for Best Picture, and the American Film Institute declared *Pulp Fiction* one of the 100 greatest American films ever made. At this point, no matter what he does, Quentin Tarantino has secured his legacy as one of the greatest filmmakers in the history of cinema.

As such, it's important to film scholarship to document his evolution as both a writer and director. Countless books and articles have been devoted to Tarantino and his professional film output, but very little has been written about his earlier pre-*Reservoir Dogs* projects. (In most volumes, *My Best Friend's Birthday* is covered in just a page or two, making this book easily the most comprehensive look at the film to date.)

A fellow writer commented to me about how ridiculous he felt the idea of a full volume on this film was, but I disagree. While I agree that in its current state, *My Best Friend's Birthday* is more of a curiosity than anything else, and even if it had been completed the way Tarantino and crew had envisioned it, it would never have stood as an equal beside the likes of *Reservoir Dogs* or *Pulp Fiction*, I think it's tremendously important in terms of what it represents in terms of film scholarship.

Examining the film and the process in which it was made (at least what was completed) allows us to see the earliest stages of an artist learning his craft and finding his voice. Certainly there are elements of the Tarantino style we would see in his later films, and it's fascinating to see the evolution of his art from his beginnings through to his latest project, *Once Upon a Time in Hollywood*. There is tremendous growth over that span, as one would expect from any artist of merit, but it's clear that the talent was always present. At the time of *My Best Friend's Birthday*, that talent was still rough. It needed honing, just as the earliest works of any artist do. No great artist emerges from the womb fully formed.

Beyond charting the artist's evolution, *My Best Friend's Birthday: The Making of a Quentin Tarantino Film* is a story about a group of friends who shared a passion for film and came together to try to make their own. And within that story is another: the story of two friends, Quentin Tarantino and Craig Hamann, who shared a singular dream. They set out to make that dream a reality, watching a few films and having some adventures along the way, and the end result is the making (or attempted making) of *My Best Friend's Birthday*.

The structure of this book is unorthodox, but again, I wanted this book to more than a simple documentation of the film. Because of this, it is divided into three sections. The first, "The Pieces Come Together," focuses on how each of the primary players involved with the film met and came together. (This is also the most comprehensive look at Tarantino's acting school days and famed Video Archives period to date.) The second section, "Making Movies," focuses on the nuts and bolts of no-budget filmmaking. It's not just about the making of *My Best Friend's Birthday*, but also an earlier film, *Warzone*, which paved the way. Like *Birthday*, *Warzone* also remains unfinished. As it was neither written nor directed by

Tarantino, it is included here simply to document the progression of the crew's shooting methods. If *My Best Friend's Birthday* was Tarantino and company's film school, then *Warzone* must be seen as a sort of preparatory school. Section three, "Script and Film Breakdown," was designed to provide readers with an idea of what the completed film might have looked like. For this, I closely examined the screenplay and the half hour of footage that's available. I also break down the scenes, providing accompanying trivia and background. There is also a running commentary by the film's co-writer, producer, and second lead Craig Hamann, in which he and others discuss the ideas behind the characters and scenes, as well as details regarding the shoot.

I tried to reach everyone involved with this film. Some called back, and some didn't. For a long time, I didn't think I would get Tarantino for this book. I contacted his agent Mike Simpson a dozen times, but received no response. (This occurs frequently when dealing with agents and publicists, causing one to question their purpose and efficiency.) Then Tarantino responded to a personal message on April 10, 2018—literally five minutes before I received the call telling me to come to the hospital for my heart transplant—informing me he was aware of the project. But then I went into the hospital for several months, and nothing came of Tarantino's reaching out. I eventually gave up hope and wrote an (earlier) introduction (incorrectly) explaining why I felt Tarantino might be distancing himself from *My Best Friend's Birthday*, and why he shouldn't. In that earlier piece, I compared the film to Stanley Kubrick's early effort *Fear and Desire*, which Kubrick attempted to bury.

But then in January 2019, Tarantino messaged me again and asked if I still wanted an interview. I didn't tell him I had already turned in my "completed" manuscript a few days earlier. I said yes, which any writer in this situation would. (I had met Tarantino in person way back in 1999 and had been actively trying to secure an interview with him since 1997.)

I then contacted my editor and asked the publisher to stop work on the book. Tarantino's assistant, Mayra Garcia, and I exchanged numerous messages. We set up a time for a phone interview, but Tarantino was a no show. Then the following night I was out of town on a date and missed an impromptu call. Two nights later, he called again—another unscheduled and unexpected call—when I was driving on the highway and had no means to record our conversation. I had to reschedule. During all of this, Tarantino was busy in full-day editing sessions on *Once Upon a Time in Hollywood*, so I wasn't sure I would get the interview.

But then, finally, on February 5, 2019, he called and asked if we could speak later in the evening. True to his word, he called and we had a terrific interview. He laughed for the duration of the conversation, and thanked me for guiding him on this trip down memory lane. He also assured me that I was wrong and that, despite all previous indications to the contrary, he did not wish to hide *My Best Friend's Birthday*. "I'm not trying to distance myself from the movie," he said. "I think it looks very amateurish and it is what it is—a student film. But it was a lovely time in my life. It was my film school." When we talked, he only had a limited amount of time, so there were things we couldn't get to. For instance, I would have loved to have talked to him about his reportedly attacking a Video Archives customer, as well as his thoughts on some of his past collaborators believing he ripped off Craig Hamann. For the record, Hamann says he doesn't agree with this assertion. But Tarantino did speak to me for the book and he was gracious despite his hectic schedule, and this book is much better as a result. (I hated the thought of writing an oral history about a Tarantino film without Tarantino himself being a part of it.)

When people see the rough footage of *My Best Friend's Birthday* that appears on the Internet—tenth generation reproductions from old VHS tapes—they frequently remark about its amateurish nature. But it's important to remember that this was a black-and-white film made for $5,000 utilizing mostly amateur actors and crew members. With its scant budget and intermittent shooting manner, there was no way the film could have been anything more. No matter how primitive *My Best Friend's Birthday* might look, the screenplay which frames it (co-written by Tarantino and Hamann) is remarkable. As discussed elsewhere in this volume, the script isn't hampered by the compromised locations, acting missteps, and rookie filmmaking mistakes that occasionally appear in the film.

After shelving *My Best Friend's Birthday*, Tarantino moved on to work on bigger and better things. It has been heavily discussed that elements of *My Best Friend's Birthday* appear in later projects. Character names are repeated and sometimes dialogue is reused verbatim, but every writer in every medium cannibalizes elements from their unseen works. There are always elements of an unpublished or unfilmed writing by talented scribes that are qualitative enough to demand repurposing.

I chose the format of the book because I've always loved oral histories. This *Rashomon* style allows multiple characters/participants to share their perspectives and show us how they viewed the events in their own words. Because of the nature of the human brain and memory being untrustworthy, every person remembers an event as occurring in a slightly different way. Sometimes the disparity is in the tiniest of details, but at other times stories will be significantly different.

Who is telling the truth? Or, more to the point, who remembers correctly? The truth likely lies somewhere in the middle. It has been said that there is no such thing as an entirely accurate depiction of any event, and the oral history presentation frequently proves this. However, the format is effective because it allows each person to provide his or her own version of the truth, leaving the reader to consider what they've read and then determine what they believe to be true.

In compiling this book, I tried to be as impartial as possible. This book was written as a celebration of Tarantino and his work, but there are occasionally things stated by participants that may be seen as unflattering. I felt it was important that the work not be compromised by withholding such details, statements, and assessments. I worked hard to be as honest and thorough in the depictions of events as possible, so those stories and accounts are included here, warts and all.

— ANDREW J. RAUSCH

THE *SHOCK CINEMA* "ROSETTA STONE" REVIEW
from issue #22, Spring/Summer 2003
by Steve Puchalski

The trailers for *Kill Bill* proudly proclaim that it's Quentin Tarantino's fourth film. Technically, that's correct, because nobody would consider his first, uncompleted 16mm project (made when he was still clerking at Video Archives) to be a finished work. This black-and-white screwball comedy was written by Tarantino and acting-class comrade Craig Hamann, photographed by Roger Avary, and funded by his video store pals. But after numerous technical problems, Quentin scrapped the project and moved on to bigger and better things. After all these years, thirty-seven minutes of this legendary film have finally surfaced. At first glance, it's just a bunch of jumbled scenes, as crude as any Richard Kern flick, with comedy that rivals *Meatballs Part II*. But when it was over, I was hooked. I wanted to see more of these eccentric characters, as they dealt with love, loss, potential violence, and their unending obsession with the movies. Most of the footage is from early portions of the film, beginning with a shockingly young Quentin (sporting Stray Cats hand-me-downs) as motor-mouthed radio DJ Clarence Pool, who recalls how—at the tender age of three—he was saved from suicide by the Partridge Family. But when Clarence snorts a baggie full of coke during a commercial break, he has an on-air meltdown. In another subplot, Mickey (Craig Hamann, who directed the 1997 Marc Dacascos thriller *Boogie Boy*) discovers his ex-girlfriend in his apartment and is thrilled—until he learns that she's just there to collect her shit and has a new Yuppie boyfriend. Meanwhile, it's poor rejected Mickey's birthday and Clarence, his best friend, needs a suitable present. How about hiring a novice call girl named Misty (Crystal Shaw, who went on to write and star in the 1998 short film *Have a Periwinkle Day*)? These scenes might be raw and disconnected, but they also display the same snappy dialogue and oddball characters that energize Tarantino's current work. In fact, this often seems like the Rosetta Stone of his future career. All of the influences and answers are here, crammed together into one big hodgepodge. There are obscure film references galore, Aldo Ray jokes, discussions about the genius of De Palma, Clarence's foot fetish confession, and Quentin gives himself a romantic scene with Misty, whose career choice was inspired by Nancy Allen's whore in *Dressed to Kill!* Allen Garfield (who was Tarantino's acting teacher at his Beverly Hills' Acting Shelter) turns up as a bakery owner, when Clarence buys a cake for Mickey and argues about Elvis Presley's limited acting abilities. Plus, a background one-sheet collection includes cool, cult-movie faves like *The Fury, Chato's Land, Black Oak Conspiracy, Squirm,* and (of course) a Sonny Chiba flick. He even squeezes in a lame martial arts showdown between Mickey and Misty's black pimp, Clifford, and includes background tunes like "Ballroom Blitz" (long before Quentin could actually afford to buy the rights).

PART ONE

INTRODUCTION: BE YOUR OWN FILM SCHOOL
by Kieran Fisher

Every filmmaker needs to start somewhere. Some spend years in film school learning all there is to know about the craft before they feel equipped enough to embark on their own cinematic journey. Others spend years working on sets as coffee-makers and grips and cinematographers and assistant directors and whatnot before they take the directorial reins themselves. Then you have the self-taught DIY auteurs who learn simply by picking up a camera and practicing until they find their groove. The latter tend to have the most fascinating backstories.

Quentin Tarantino's journey from video store clerk to self-taught writer/director is well documented. Consuming cinema—from seminal masterworks to micro-budget schlock and everything in between—studying movies frame by frame, learning all there was to know about the players involved, writing his own screenplays, and eventually picking up the camera, was his film school. The Deuce's path is nothing short of inspirational to anyone who's ever dreamed of creating art of any kind, as his rags-to-riches story instills a belief and optimism that any average joe can create something that resonates with people if they put the time and effort into honing their craft.

These days, whether you love his work or absolutely loathe it, Tarantino occupies a special place in Hollywood as a successful one-of-a-kind maverick. His style is distinct, and he's been able to ascend the film industry marching to the beat of his own drum. Isn't that the dream for every aspiring filmmaker?

This has been the case for the entirety of his career, too. From the get-go, it was evident that Tarantino had one thing every artist must possess to stand out from the overcrowded pack: a voice. The most valuable skill storytellers have is their voice, and if they can figure out a way to articulate it through the language of cinema, they have more chance of being noticed. The opening scenes in *My Best Friend's Birthday*, which feature Tarantino waxing lyrical about suicide and sitcoms, aren't his most polished by any means. They do, however, instantly showcase the snappy dialogue, random pop culture references, and offbeat humorous qualities that have since informed all of his films to some extent. To put it simply: you know *My Best Friend's Birthday* is a Quentin Tarantino film.

Of course, there's no denying that *My Best Friend's Birthday* is awkward and amateurish. The voice that changed the face of American cinema during the '90s is there, but you could say that it was having difficulty articulating itself. The young Tarantino was so innocent and vulnerable here, too, which is quite a contrast to the bravado he demonstrated walking next to Harvey Keitel, Steve Buscemi, Michael Madsen, and other acting heavyweights in the opening scene of *Reservoir Dogs*. It's most certainly a far cry from the self-assured, confident voice who interrupted *The Hateful Eight* to directly address the audience with an unexpected narration, reminding us that we were watching a Quentin Tarantino movie, as if we needed reminding in the first place.

That said, Tarantino's films have always boasted bags of unabashed confidence and swagger; he knows how good they are. It's part of their appeal. Even *My Best Friend's Birthday* contains that cooler-than-thou attitude that permeates his entire oeuvre, even if doesn't compare to the quality of his subsequent efforts. But that in itself is also charming, if you ask me. The fact that *My Best Friend's Birthday* hints at his bravado and genius without actually backing it up per se is a reminder that one of the best filmmakers of all time was just a young buck who, once upon a time, was trying to find his way.

Still, regardless of how one enters the business, most filmmakers fail before they succeed. Sure, some of them make sure their introductions to the world are the most professional and sophisticated efforts they can be. It's also rare to meet an artist or creator of any kind who hasn't been critical toward or embarrassed by some of their work from time to time. Perhaps this is why Tarantino hasn't had nice things to say about his unfinished debut throughout the years. However, in spite of all the messy and disjointed elements of *My*

Best Friend's Birthday, not to mention the lack of an ending, it's a fascinating little oddity nonetheless.

Like Andrew Rausch, my own professional endeavors can be traced back to seeing *Pulp Fiction* for the first time and feeling inspired by it. That was the film that made me want to learn more about cinema beyond what was on the screen. I became obsessed with Tarantino's work, and the films he cited as influences were my gateway to what's been an obsession with cinema as a whole ever since. Many of my peers and colleagues had a similar reaction to his work during their early days as budding film fanatics, and so did many of the top filmmakers and artists working today.

The cultural impact of Quentin Tarantino cannot be overstated. Of course, *My Best Friend's Birthday* is rarely hailed as the Tarantino movie that blew the collective minds of his fanbase, but I wouldn't be surprised to learn that this amateurish curiosity has inspired some dreamers to write a script, round up some friends, rent a camera, and create their first attempt at a movie.

Here we have a film that was made for pocket change, shot in a video store, and starred a group of buddies who just wanted to make a movie because they loved the art of cinema and had to make their own contribution to the field. And maybe the film they produced was amateurish and flawed, but to dismiss it as meritless or something that deserves to be forgotten is a narrow-minded view.

For a start, it's not nearly as bad as Tarantino and other naysayers would have you believe. There's plenty of clever dialogue and flashes of the genius that we now know as Tarantino. But the most important thing to take away from *My Best Friend's Birthday* is that stumbling blocks can be overcome; if you persevere and don't let your failures drag you down, one day you might get to make your own *Reservoir Dogs*. Who knows? Maybe one day you'll become an influential figure to all the artists who are just starting out and experiencing their own grind—the same types of artists all our favorite creative types were at some stage in their lives.

With this in mind, a book dedicated to this early chapter of Tarantino's career is long overdue. Whether you're a connoisseur of film history, a creator, a fan of the Deuce's movies, a keen reader, or a combination of all of the above, you're about to gain plenty of knowledge about a film that's never been covered this substantially before. There's also no one better to document this era of Tarantino's career than Mr. Rausch, and the interviewees he assembled to share their experiences offer a variety of fascinating perspectives about the film and Tarantino himself. Enjoy.

— KIERAN FISHER is a writer from Glasgow, Scotland who can be found at *Film School Rejects/One Perfect Shot, Diabolique Magazine,* and *Arrow Video*. When he's not writing about movies, he spends the majority of his free time watching and thinking about them. He can also be found all over the internet talking about how perfect *Goodfellas* is to anyone who'll listen.

THE PIECES COME TOGETHER

The story of *My Best Friend's Birthday* begins with a pair of wannabe actors who met and became best friends while studying at the James Best Theater Center in Toluca Lake in January 1981. The two new friends, Quentin Tarantino and Craig Hamann, were studying under journeyman actor James Best, whose former students included Gary Busey, Lindsay Wagner, Jerry Seinfeld, and Terri Garr. Best's acting career had begun as a contract player at Universal Studios way back in 1949. He had appeared in everything from *Gunsmoke* to the Budd Boetticher western *Ride Lonesome*, but would ultimately be remembered for playing bumbling Sheriff Rosco P. Coltrane on *The Dukes of Hazzard*.

CRAIG HAMANN (co-writer, actor, producer): James Best did a lot of quality work, and he acted during a time when macho, hard-drinking, two-fisted actors roamed the industry. Quentin and I both had tremendous respect for James Best's acting skills.

RICHARD "RICK" SQUERI (classmate): Jimmy had a long career and he'd been in a lot of wonderful things years before that had big names. He was a cocky guy in person. He wasn't quite as "aw shucks" and nice as some of the characters he played. He had a real edge to him in person.

Shortly after being cast on *The Dukes of Hazzard*, Best had decided to establish his own school for actors. Best's business partner, Jack Lucarelli, owned and operated a blue jean shop located directly across the street from the Honey Baked Ham Deli and Grill Restaurant at 10106 Riverside Drive. Best and Lucarelli rented out the space upstairs above Honey Baked Ham, where they began to operate the James Best Theater Center in 1979. (As a humorous aside, many years later when Tarantino would cast his acting coach, Brenda Hillhouse, in a minor role in *Pulp Fiction*, the two would attempt to explain the way they'd met to Christopher Walken. Walken found it amusing. "So, let me get this straight," he would say, chuckling. "This was your acting teacher, and the two of you met in an acting school that was upstairs above a ham store? Well, now that makes perfect sense!")

Being situated above a ham store wasn't the only thing that made the James Best Theater Center different from other acting schools. According to Hillhouse, who served as the school's beginning acting teacher, the school's focus was different, too.

BRENDA HILLHOUSE (teacher): When Jimmy Best was coming up as an actor, things were very different from a technical standpoint. Actors needed to know how to protect themselves in front of the camera. They needed to know how to position themselves in group scenes so they'd be next to the money. That way if they had to do coverage they'd get to work more. Jimmy also taught how to scale down what you were doing in your characterization so it was more realistic and less theatrical. That was primarily his technique. It was not about acting.

Jimmy's primary focus was teaching how to do your best on camera and make it impossible for them to cut you out. As a day player, you'd get one, maybe two shots, and then the rest of the time you're reading off camera with the star. So, Jimmy's technique was about allowing actors to take advantage of every opportunity they had, pulling focus to them, and making sure their one take was the absolute best it could be. He also taught students not to be intimidated. Actors coming out of school are used to having had ample time to prepare, and they've rehearsed in a theatre-type setting. Then they get hired as a day player and they show up on set. They don't know anybody, and now they've got sixteen grips and cameramen all around them. As an actor, that's your first shot, and you're completely thrown by all of that. And you might not get another shot. So that was Jimmy's reason for starting the school.

DAVID O'HARA (classmate): Looking back on it now, the class was kind of a joke. A guy named Jack Lucarelli ran it. He was one of the worst actors on the planet. Believe it or not, he was stiffer than Chuck Norris, which puts him very close to a block of granite. Their thing that they were teaching was called "camera technique." You didn't have to know how to act, as long as you knew how to hit your marks and stand still, say your lines, you know? I think the class basically was a little ego thing for James Best. He would show up a couple times a year, so everyone could kiss the ring.

He decided he was going to put on the play *Orpheus Descending* by Tennessee Williams. The lead in that is a guy around twenty-eight or thirty-ish. They were casting all the roles in class, and I was waiting for them to cast the lead, Jabe Torrance. They get all the casting done for the whole play, and I say, "Hey Jack! You left out the lead." And he says, "Oh, Jimmy's going to play that." *He was in his fifties!* "Yeah, but he wants to play it…" So, then they got into rehearsals, and that went on for a couple of weeks. Everybody learning their lines and stuff, actually working on it. Jimmy never showed up for any of the rehearsals. And then the play just disappeared… Jimmy never bothered to tell anyone that he changed his mind and that they weren't going to do it. He let all these people do this work, which in his mind was okay. He is a good actor, he's done some very good work, but that's just something I was scratching my head at.

Hillhouse interviewed would-be student Tarantino in 1980. The school had a strict policy that insisted students must be at least eighteen years old to attend classes. Tarantino, who had just dropped out of high school and was only seventeen at the time, lied and said he was nineteen.

BRENDA HILLHOUSE: Quentin had tracked Jimmy Best down because a lot of actors that Quentin liked—especially Gary Busey—had studied with him.

What I remember about Quentin was that he was incredibly earnest. He was also passionately in love with anything having to do with film and television and acting. He was very humble, and just very thrilled to be given a shot to work with Jimmy. At the time he was living in Manhattan Beach, and he would ride the bus all the way out to Toluca Lake to come to class two or three times a week. I always thought Quentin was like a little puppy dog. He was just so sweet and so earnest, so in love with anything and everything about acting. But back then, if you had asked me if Quentin would be the guy who made it big from that group, I don't think I would have said yes. And that's just because he was a little nerdy and a little bit different. He was a little bit out on the edge. But you know what? When I look back now, I realize those were exactly the things that propelled him to where he is now.

JACK LUCARELLI (teacher): Quentin had dropped out of high school. He told his mom he was gonna come to Hollywood. He said he'd considered theatre down in Torrance, California, but in local communities you're not gonna get the right kind of training. And I don't believe you can get it in college. So, he came to Hollywood, and being the super fan he was, and having the mind he had—I think he's watched about every movie in the history of movies—he was a fan of James Best. So, he came to our theater.

I was auditioning people because Jimmy was off working on *Dukes of Hazzard*, and in comes this kid. There was just something about him that I took to, just that quirkiness, that kookiness. He had an overwhelming passion and desire, and I could feel that. Right from the get-go, I thought this was a guy, I don't know how, where, why, when, but I knew something was gonna happen for this guy. So, my gut feeling ended up being right. And I have nothing but respect for a man who wanted something that bad and didn't give up until he achieved it.

Quentin was kind of a homeless dude at the time. He didn't have the funds, so I let him sleep at the workshop sometimes. I would have let him stay forever. He was loyal and he was a good student. The workshop upstairs above Honey Baked Hams was his bedroom. Then he'd go across the street to a restaurant and take a bath in the sink. Then he'd get on a bus—maybe two or three buses—and he'd go downtown and watch a couple of movies and then ride all those buses back to Toluca Lake. He became really well acquainted with the area. He knew Toluca Lake better than any of us. The thing about Quentin is, he paid his dues, and no one can say otherwise.

Quentin is the real deal. He was in it for all the right reasons. He was unique. I recognized the talent. Years later, it was very enlightening when he told me that he was in it because he loved cinema. Those were his exact words. Too many people are in it for the wrong reasons—fame, fortune, attention. But he was true to himself all the way through. He said, "Jack, I just want you to know the reason I was there was because I love cinema." And I look back, and for all those who didn't make it and Quentin did, he made it because he was pure. He was a good kid, and he deserves everything he's achieved.

CONNIE ZASTOUPIL (Tarantino's mother): I wasn't at all put off by the idea of Quentin going to the acting school, and I had a vague notion of who James Best was. I knew him a little bit from the movies. I felt like that would be a good experience for him. He doesn't believe I was very supportive, but I was as supportive as I could be with the knowledge of how difficult it was to succeed in Hollywood. He had to ride a bus quite a distance to get to the theater, because I wouldn't let him have a car at that time. But I did the same thing when I was in college and I was very young, so I felt like that was a good experience for him.

In his 2009 memoir, *Best in Hollywood: The Good, the Bad, and the Beautiful*, James Best discussed Tarantino's time at the school:

Quentin walked into my class one day and said, "Mr. Best, I want to meet you. You worked in my favorite movie of all time."

"Really? What's that?" I asked.

"Rolling Thunder."

"Rolling Thunder?" I asked. I had played such a mean person in that film. I turned the part down three times before I finally accepted it. They kept raising the money to where I finally rationalized that it was okay to prostitute my integrity for that

much money, so I did it. Tommy Lee Jones and William Devane also were given enough reasons to appear in the film.

Quentin started quoting lines from the picture. Then, he mentioned other movies that I made and quoted dialogue from them, too. What a memory he had.... He obviously liked movies of all kinds.

When Quentin got onstage in class, he was less than adequate. I told Jack Lucarelli: "Throw him out. Get him out of the school. He's a terrible actor."

Jack said, "The poor guy hasn't got any money. He sleeps in the theater once in a while because he doesn't even have enough money for bus fare."

"Oh. Well, hell. Let him stay."

I went to Quentin and told him, "You're a lousy actor. You should take up writing."

Despite Best's disregard for Tarantino, the former student maintained a deep respect for him and would later offer him a role in a 1996 film he produced called *Curdled*. "I read the gory, blood-soaked script, and I concluded that it was absolute trash, and I presumed that it would never make any money." Although Tarantino had offered Best the role as a gesture of respect, Best balked, expressing anger at being offered scale. "I haven't worked for minimum in fifty years, and I'm not about to start again, especially with a guy who doesn't know diddly squat about directing," Best would remark. "The fact that Quentin had been nominated two years earlier for an Academy Award as Best Director and had won an Academy Award for writing *Pulp Fiction* did not make me change my mind. I was so amazed by his success that I scratched my head and wondered, 'Where the hell did he learn to direct?'" Best would go on to criticize his most famous pupil, saying, "I am correct about stating that Quentin cannot act." Best would begrudgingly admit that Tarantino was a "major talent and a keen creative force who has helped keep the edges sharp in filmmaking," but then immediately follow that statement by taking another shot: "[H]e is one of a kind. Thank goodness our planet has room for only one of him."

BRENDA HILLHOUSE: Jimmy was an artist and all that goes with that, meaning that he was often cantankerous. He came up in the industry as a contract player at Universal, during a time in the '50s and '60s when being a man in the industry meant your day rate was sort of your measure of worth. There was always a sensitivity to him, a fear that people were going to take advantage of him. So, offering him scale to do something was seen as a huge insult.

JACK LUCARELLI: If I had made a movie at the time, and I've produced a few now, I'd have had to offer Jimmy scale to appear in it, too. Sometimes the money just isn't there. That's in no way a knock to the actor, it's just the reality; you can't offer them money that isn't there. I think the fact that Quentin couldn't pay Jimmy the kind of money he was used to getting upset him. And Jimmy had a short fuse sometimes. He was a great guy and I loved him to death, but sometimes things got under his skin. But Quentin certainly didn't mean it as a slight. He loved Jimmy and was in awe of him. That's why he offered him that role in the first place. Quentin was pure and he had good motives. Jimmy just took that the wrong way.

And look, there may have been a little envy there. Quentin has achieved everything that anyone who wants to be a writer, director, actor, or producer wants in this business. Jimmy had his fair share of fame and respect as an actor, but what Quentin has achieved is extraordinary. It's extraordinary by anyone's standards.

BRENDA HILLHOUSE: Quentin was not the best actor in the class, but if Jimmy ever had that conversation about throwing him out of the class, I was not privy to it. It makes sense that Jack would have defended Quentin, because he, like I, always had a fondness for him. Also, it wasn't so much that Quentin couldn't afford bus fare to get home, but often our classes and the ensuing late-night get togethers afterwards would stretch past the time for the last bus back to Manhattan Beach. Because of that, he wouldn't have a place to sleep on those nights. So Jack would let him sleep in the theater.

CRAIG HAMANN: Quentin and I both had the utmost respect for James Best, and that's the truth. But he seemed surprisingly unappreciative of the film history he had helped make; things like *Rolling Thunder*, which Quentin and I greatly admired.

BRENDA HILLHOUSE: I think Quentin appreciated Jimmy's vast amount of work, because he was obsessed and well-versed with these movies. I remember Quentin talking about Jimmy's part in *Shenandoah*, and him getting shot in the forehead on the battlefield. He was fascinated with Jimmy, and with all character actors, really. Allen Garfield is another person he would later study with. And then there are all of the people like Michael Parks whom he's cast in his movies over the years.

QUENTIN TARANTINO: James Best was always extremely nice to me, but the reality is this: maybe I saw James Best eight times ever, at the most. And he never saw me act. Not once. The thing is, it was really Jack Lucarelli's class. Jack had been James' student a long time ago. And when Jack had *Dukes of Hazzard*, he was doing great. So they started this school. Jimmy was initially going to be more involved with it, but then that just wasn't the case. But of course it wasn't gonna be the case! He was working on a fucking TV show! He had more money than he'd ever had in his life *and* he had this big TV show. And that's hard work. So really, they were just using Jimmy's name. Jimmy was like the godfather of the place, but really it was Jack's school. It was Jack's class and Jack was the one paying the rent. Jack was the one who had the building and Jack was the one teaching the students. Jimmy would show up every once in a great while and just give a lecture on what it was like to be a working actor on an episodic television guest shot. But Jimmy never saw me act. If I hadn't become famous, he wouldn't have remembered me at all. I'll bet he didn't remember me even when I became famous. I think Jack told him who I was. And I'm sure Jack said, "Remember, he was the kid who loved *Rolling Thunder*?"

Craig Hamann first attended class after being invited by Jack Lucarelli's wife, Jeannie Wilson, who'd met him as a customer at Bank of America, where Hamann was working as a teller.

JEANNIE WILSON: That was the bank Jack and I went to. After a while, you get to kind of know the tellers. So one day I was in there and we were just kind of talking and Craig mentioned he was an actor. I said, "You are? Well, we have an acting school. You should come to it."

BRENDA HILLHOUSE: Jeannie said Craig was so damned gorgeous that she figured he was an actor. So then he came and joined the class.

Although much has been written about Hamann's anger issues as a young man, his friend and classmate Rick Squeri shares a softer story regarding his first encounter with him. Hamann had just performed in front of the class and had been heavily criticized by Lucarelli. Hamann then retreated to the bathroom, where he became upset and started questioning his abilities. Squeri, still a stranger at this point, recognized that Hamann was hurting and stepped in to calm him. "I gave him a big hug and said, 'Dude, it's gonna be okay,'" recalls Squeri. Tarantino would eventually make his way into the bathroom, as well, assisting Squeri in his support of Hamann. The three classmates soon became friends.

RICHARD "RICK" SQUERI: It was kind of obvious that Quentin and Craig were folks who were in that same kind of different thinking realm I was in. They felt more like friends of mine than a lot of the other folks there. They felt more like people I had grown up with. There was a familiarity and also a wonderful kinship, which was giving each other a hard time sarcastically and in good humor.

Because of Jimmy's orientation and what was being shown on television at the time, they were interested in promoting a lot more *Dukes of Hazzard* kind of guys and gals. It wasn't necessarily a breeding ground for them, but that was sort of the eye they used to look at things.

CRAIG HAMANN: I really enjoyed watching what Quentin was doing. He was, without a doubt, one of the most creative people in the class.

DAVID O'HARA: Back then, Quentin was the last person in that class you would have thought would end up working in this business. But he was the only one in that class that did anything, and he made a giant success of himself. He still can't act though. He was the worst actor in *Pulp Fiction*.

BRENDA HILLHOUSE: Quentin and Craig did a lot of their scenes together. We were doing a lot of showcases for casting directors. They were always great at helping out behind the scenes, doing the music cues, and all that sort of stuff, because it was usually people from the advanced classes that were featured in the showcases. Quentin and Craig were young, interested, and hopeful.

Students were asked to find dramatic scenes and bring them to perform in class. According to Hillhouse, Tarantino and Hamann were "much more interested in movies," and eventually grew tired of performing classic theatre material. It was then the two began crafting their own scenes, many of which came from movies.

CRAIG HAMANN: When Quentin and I did scenes, most of the time they were scenes I had written. After a while, Quentin started writing scenes as well. We also performed a lot of scenes from cooler B-movies, while everyone else was doing mainstream Hollywood film and TV scenes.

QUENTIN TARANTINO: Everybody else in the class would go to Samuel French and get scenes. They would do scenes from plays. God, I can't remember how many times I saw the confrontation scene from *The Turning Point*. It was like every two gals in the class had to do that at least once. I got so sick of that scene!

I wanted to do movie scenes, but scripts weren't readily available in those days. But I was going to movies all the fucking time, and I didn't want to just do normal theatrical stuff. I wanted to do wild stuff—the kind of scenes you wouldn't see in an acting class. So I would go to the movies and I would see a scene and I'd say, "This would be a great scene for class." And the thing is, I have a really good memory. So I would go home and write the scene down from memory. Jack Lucarelli would say, "If you like the scene from a movie you should go buy a novelization of it." But I didn't do that. I just remembered it. I'd write it from memory. And if there was anything I didn't remember, or if anything came to me while I was writing, I would just add. That's how I started writing dialogue. I did a scene from Dino DeLaurentiis' *Flash Gordon*; I did a scene from Jackie Chan's *The Big Brawl*; I did a scene from *Paradise Alley*... You know, all the cool movies from that time period.

JACK LUCARELLI: We encouraged people to write their own scenes. So, Quentin apparently saw a Paddy Chayefsky movie. He said he went home and he remembered every word of the dialogue, which blows my mind.

BRENDA HILLHOUSE: Quentin would go to a movie theater, take a little flashlight, and scribble down the dialogue from movies that he liked. Then he would bring that in to perform in class.

One day he was doing a scene from the movie *Marty*. The scene started out like the movie, but then it wandered way the hell over into the weeds. I said, "Wait a minute, I thought you said this was from *Marty*?" And he said, "I couldn't write fast enough, so I just made the rest of it up." I said, "Well, keep making it up." The stuff he had written was really good.

QUENTIN TARANTINO: I decided to do a scene from *Marty*, but I didn't have *Marty* to go from, so I just had to remember what the scene was. So I wrote that down, and then I did the scene with Ronny Coleman.

A few years later, me and Ronny were roommates in Hawthorne. We were talking one day and I was telling him, "After writing those scenes in class, I think I have a pretty good handle on writing dialogue." And he said, "What do you mean 'have a handle on writing dialogue'? You're as good as Paddy Chayefsky!" I said, "What the fuck do you mean?" He said, "Do you remember when we did that scene from *Marty*?" I said yeah, and he said, "Well, you wrote it out and you gave it to me. I actually had a copy of *Marty*, so I compared it to the original Paddy Chayefsky script, and you added an entire monologue about a fountain. And it was just as good as anything else in the scene. It completely meshed with Paddy Chayefsky's dialogue and it didn't stand out. You would have thought it was part of *Marty*." And it wasn't until that moment that Ronny Coleman said that to me that I started to take my writing seriously. And when he said that to me, I was like, "Hmm, maybe I should be more serious about this. Maybe he has a point here. Maybe this shouldn't just be stuff for us to do in acting class. Maybe it should be something else." That was literally the moment I started taking my writing seriously.

CRAIG HAMANN: Quentin would add his own take on scenes from movies, or would combine a couple of scenes. I was doing the same thing. It was really fun doing scenes that we had written. Even then we were very serious about making our own movie one day. I wrote scenes from a few film ideas we had. Keep in mind that was as close as we got to having the scenes be seen by anyone. We would do the scenes, get the feedback from Jimmy or Jack, and then access the scenes ourselves. I would say that creatively those days were some of the most fun I ever had.

QUENTIN TARANTINO: Craig had written this dystopian future script called *Thanatos: The Last Quest*. There was me, Rick Squeri, and Brenda Peters. And basically, we would just do different scenes from Craig's script every other week in class. So eventually we kind of got to see the whole movie.

RICHARD "RICK" SQUERI: We did a scene where a guy wakes up in a cellar and he's handcuffed to a pipe. There's a guy who's got a gun on him, and I think he's got a bomb set. He tells the guy about how tough the handcuffs are and says, "Here's a hacksaw. If you start right now, you can saw through those handcuffs in nine-point-eight minutes. But the bomb's going to go off in seven. But if you choose to saw off your hand, you can do that in five." It was that kind of stuff, which was right up our alley. We just loved that stuff. It was fun and it challenged emotions and got us going. It was also the kind of thing that wasn't seen as being a very good thing to bring to the James Best Theater Center.

It was obvious that the three of us weren't going to fit in with this kind of good ol' boy romantic fun stuff. They would talk about things like Robert De Niro, but they really had no idea what kind of different perspective that entailed. They were really formulaic in the projects we would read together or the kinds of scripts they would look at. They just couldn't see things this other way or see why it would be popular. What we were bringing was distasteful to them. It wasn't recognized as something that was different good, it was different bad. They loved to dabble with edgy subjects, but they never challenged anything. It was go to the formula, get the formula going, and make the picture.

The group was so committed to their performance of these scenes that they eventually brought actual guns to class for use as props. "The guns were unloaded, of course," explains Hamann. Some rememeber Tarantino as being part of the scene, but this was not the case.

QUENTIN TARANTINO: I wasn't in the scene with the guns. It was Rick and Brenda and Craig. I remember thinking it was the only time I'd been in class where I felt the actors were creating a shock, as opposed to just standing in front of the class and doing a scene. It started out with an empty stage, which no one ever did unless it opened with someone opening a door. And then Craig walked in with a shotgun! And he starts loading the shotgun. And then Rick walks in with an automatic rifle! First there was one person on stage, and now there are two people on stage loading their weapons. And then Brenda Peters walks on and she's loading her Magnum.

They weren't loading them with real bullets or anything, but they were real guns. But you could just feel the shock in the room. They entered the scene and they were gonna go out and kick some ass. It was the coolest opening I'd ever seen in an acting class, and I spent years in acting classes. I thought, "This could be a scene in a movie! This isn't just acting class bullshit!"

RICHARD "RICK" SQUERI: Jack was an aficionado of firearms, so we knew he would need to see the guns in advance and look them over. I remember Jack saying, "*Whoa! Whoa! I need to check those out!*" And we knew when we came in, he was going to ask that. He examined them and was kind of talking to us about them, letting us know he knew about guns.

JACK LUCARELLI: I grew up around guns. I'd been around guns my whole life. When those weapons came out, I got pissed. I thought, if you're gonna pull something like that, don't do it for shock value. I think I was probably mostly angry about the lack of respect and concern for the rest of the class they had shown. And I do believe when they did that, it was done for shock value. They must have thought it was fun and games and funny. It wasn't funny to me.

RICHARD "RICK" SQUERI: I think that was probably the most well-armed scene ever done there. It consisted of a Mausberg shotgun, Craig had an M-16-style rifle, and there were a couple of handguns. It just added gravitas to the scene. I remember there were people in the class who were a little bit nervous about that, and we assured them there was nothing to be concerned about. We brought them in their cases. It wasn't as though we came in brandishing them. But almost everyone there sort of took their tone from Jack and Jimmy. That's why I said we didn't fit in. We were really kind of the misfits from the get-go.

CRAIG HAMANN: When I think back about it, we were crazy. But that's the kind of macho, B-movie stuff we did. I think we scared some of the acting class with our weirdness.

JACK LUCARELLI: Humans are always doing something. Right now I'm fiddling with my ring while I'm talking to you. But if I do that same thing onstage for effect, and it's not coming from a genuine and true place in terms of motivation, then the scene becomes about that. But it shouldn't. The scene isn't about the guns. The scene is still about the feelings. The one thing I say to actors is, if you aren't feeling it, then the audience won't feel it. That's from Stanislavski, and it's true. Your job as an actor is to think and feel and not to "act" from the head, and don't make the scene about the guns or whatever the prop is. And you know, back then, these were all guys who were fairly new to acting, so immediately the scene became about those guns.

DAVID O'HARA: I don't remember the guns, but it doesn't

surprise me that they did that. Sometimes those props are used as crutches by actors. Not even sometimes... Most of the time. They can help facilitate a scene, but if you can't do the scene without them, you're not going to be that good with them. They're not a real means to an end. They're just like having a set. That can help make it a little atmospheric, and you don't have to make up as much in your mind. Quentin and Craig and those guys, they were into that kind of stuff... Guns and macho, in-your-face scripts.

James Best would later recall Tarantino's original writing for the class:

Quentin wanted to use some of his original writings in the class.

"Why do you want to do that?" Jack asked. "Why don't you use some written material from professionals who really know how to write?"

It just goes to show that nobody at any time can predict what is good or bad. It seems that the material that Jack finally let Quentin do in that acting class was a scene that was later used in Reservoir Dogs.

CRAIG HAMANN: Quentin and I always worked together, especially in things he wrote or brought to class. I don't recall any scene from *Reservoir Dogs*, as it wasn't even written yet. Quentin wrote *Natural Born Killers* and *True Romance* before beginning on *Dogs*. And he was long gone from the acting school by that time.

After class, students and faculty would routinely go to a "bar or a Mexican restaurant" (Hillhouse) adjacent to the school to discuss movies, theatre, and the class they'd just had. Eventually the class settled into the River Bottom Inn, making it their regular after-class meeting place.

RICHARD "RICK" SQUERI: That was pretty much standard operating procedure after class. We would end up at the River Bottom Inn, which was also haunted by the actors who were coming out of the Burbank studios. These were people like John Cassavetes and Larry Pennell and Phil Everly of the Everly Brothers. There were lots and lots of actors who frequented this watering hole.

JACK LUCARELLI: Quentin later told me the reason he'd lied about his age was because he wasn't old enough to go with us to the River Bottom, and he really wanted to be there.

RICHARD "RICK" SQUERI: Quentin wasn't anywhere near old enough to drink. He was several years younger than us. We would just kind of bring him in and then act like he was old enough, so of course he would have a couple of drinks and then he became even more obnoxious than he normally was. He really got going. A number of times, he would start something with somebody and then Craig and I would have to finish what he started. That happened a couple of different times.

BRENDA HILLHOUSE: We would talk about anything and everything having to do with acting. Quentin was a go-to reference on these subjects. He knew all the names of all the actors, and he knew all the trivia. He knew all the music that was in the movies. Whenever anyone said something about this stuff, Quentin would know the real deal about it. And he was obviously very opinionated.

CRAIG HAMANN: There were a few people there who had had a film education and had seen a lot of movies. Quentin was one of them. He had clearly seen more movies than anybody else. Some of the debates guys were having were kind of strange. It was people who didn't know what they were talking about versus Quentin, who knew all of it.

JACK LUCARELLI: Anything you say to Quentin, he remembers. There was a movie called *Fort Apache, the Bronx* that Paul Newman did. Quentin and I used to have some pretty intense debates about it. I was trash talking the movie. I didn't think it was good. I love Paul Newman's work, but I thought the film really failed. So, we had a fierce debate over that because Quentin loved it. So when he reached out to me again about a year ago, out of left field, he said, "Jack, I saw *Fort Apache, the Bronx* again, and you were right. It is a piece of crap." And for Quentin to criticize a movie, there's got to be something wrong with it.

Then the reverse happened. I guess I had trashed a movie that Quentin liked. I think it was *Electra Glide in Blue*. It might have been *Tell Them Willie Boy Is Here*. I used that in conversation with Quentin as an example of great filmmaking, great acting skills. Quentin looked at me and said, "That isn't what you said back then!" So, I'll tell you what, he listens to every word and remembers.

During these after-class jaunts to the River Bottom Inn, Squeri would have some fun with his classmates, with only Hamann and Tarantino in on the bit.

CRAIG HAMANN: Rick was a stuntman back then and he would do these hilarious but real-looking pratfalls. Sometimes he'd act as if he was really drunk, even though he didn't drink all that much in reality, and run smack into a wall. It would startle people who didn't know him because he would act as if he hurt his face or whatever. Rick would make it all look so real. He would even slap the wall to make the impact sound solid. Or Rick would tumble on the street, maybe do a complete front roll, and people would freak out. It was even worse because Quentin and I would be laughing hysterically, and it would look as if we were a couple of heartless bastards.

As Tarantino and Hamann got to know one another, they found that they had many shared interests. One of these was an affinity for martial arts films. Hamann actually studied and practiced Korean, Japanese, Chinese, and Hawaiian martial arts in real life, and also dabbled in American boxing. Tarantino didn't study any martial arts, but he had an unbridled love for chop-socky flicks and Sonny Chiba imports.

CRAIG HAMANN: I had always loved movies, but Quentin started introducing me to different stuff. He would tell me I needed to see this movie or that one. I'd go out and rent it and then come back to him and say, "You were right. This is great."

One of the things he introduced me to was Chinese cinema. That included filmmakers like John Woo. He introduced me to the action movies and a few of the martial arts movies, too. I had seen quite a few Asian martial arts films before I met Quentin, but he introduced me to new things. He introduced me to Sonny Chiba, whom I hadn't been familiar with. I thought I was aware of martial arts films, but then I started talking to Mr. Encyclopedia. He's so encyclopedic about so many things when it comes to film, and he really knew his shit about martial arts films and Asian films. Being around him expanded my knowledge of those things, as well. I started renting these things, and I would also come over to his place and watch these wonderful movies with him. In that way, Quentin permanently affected me. He changed the way I look at movies, the way I write, everything. That's a big thing when you meet someone who has that kind of influence on you and can give you the kind of knowledge that stays with you for the rest of your life.

One of the movies he introduced me to was *Rolling Thunder*, which was directed by John Flynn and written by Heywood Gould and Paul Schrader. It also featured our teacher, Jimmy Best, as a bad guy. I wasn't in love with it the first time I saw it, but when I watched it the second time, I realized Quentin was right. It just knocked my socks off. I absolutely fell in love with it. That kind of violent action movie was the kind of thing the two of us loved. That movie, the Asian movies, and William Smith movies were his favorite movies at that time. William Smith was one of our favorite actors, and we both loved everything he did.

There were several Richard Gere movies he wanted me to see, that I had problems finding the energy to go see. He eventually made me come around to the point where I finally saw that Richard Gere was a talented actor. I don't know why, but I had trouble getting into him for a while. Jim McBride made a remake of Jean-Luc Godard's *Breathless* with Richard Gere, and Quentin wanted me to go see it. And I just flat out refused. I had seen the original film and I had no desire to see the remake. I didn't know who Jim McBride was, I had no interest in Valerie Kapriskie, and I didn't think Richard Gere would be good in that. We would go back and forth and he would get absolutely red in the face trying to convince me to go see it. He told me I was closed-minded.

Finally, he convinced me to go see it with him, and of course I liked it. Quentin won again!

Quentin told me one time that one of the things he liked about me was that I would say I didn't like a particular film, and he could try to make me see it differently. He would say, "The next time you see the movie, try to think about it in this way..." Then I would go see it and I would come back to him and say, "You're right. This is a good movie. I just didn't see it that way the first time." That happened a lot. I was a lot more close-minded back than I am now. Here's an ironic thing about Quentin and myself: I thought I was going to do A-list movies only, and Quentin was really into B movies. Today Quentin does A-list movies only, and I ended up making a career out of doing B movies. I don't know how we got switched around, although I know we're both happy doing what we ended up doing.

Not only did the two friends share a love of movies, but they had other things in common, as well. Both were funny, outgoing guys who dreamed of one day making a living working in film. There was an age gap between Tarantino and Hamann, who were eleven years apart, with Hamann being the elder. Hamann had written some unproduced scripts at the time, and he already had an agent, which impressed Tarantino.

Hamann hailed from Motor City, Detroit, and was the son of a big shot at the Ford Motor Company and a nurse who took care of terminally ill patients. With aspirations of breaking into film, Hamann had packed his bags and relocated to Hollywood in 1980. Hamann had a well-documented history of drug addiction, including heroin and methamphetamines. Many years later, after finding success in Hollywood, Tarantino would hire Hamann to work on *Pulp Fiction* as a technical advisor, explaining details about heroin use and overdose to Uma Thurman and John Travolta.

When Tarantino first met him, Hamann was working as a B-movie stuntman and fight coordination assistant. "I wanted to be a screenwriter, but the early jobs I got were mostly stunt work," Hamann recalls. "I got the jobs doing stunt work because I was a black belt, and they needed guys who could fight. I could do that." Hamann's movie work was intermittent, so he was supplementing his income by working as a customer service representative at Bank of America.

As stated previously, he'd had some anger issues, which had already resulted in his being kicked out of "three, maybe four" acting schools. (He would later be kicked out of the James Best Theater Center, as well.) In one incident, Hamann became enraged and started yelling at two men who were staring at him in a restaurant.

CRAIG HAMANN: I was with a photographer in a restaurant. Three guys kept eyeballing me. Being the jerk I was back then, I figured they had a problem with me. I went up to them and asked "Is there a problem?" They said no. I said, "Wise decision," and I walked away. The photographer was practically hiding beneath the table when I returned. He told me the guys were casting directors. Here I was an actor, and I had just come off as a prick to three casting directors who probably did nothing more than like my look. I probably cost myself some work as an actor.

Tarantino was a local boy (a transplant from Tennessee) who attended a private Christian school, growing up in Torrance and later El Segundo. His mother, Connie Zastoupil, was an extremely intelligent woman who has been described as a workaholic. She worked as the vice president of Cigna Health Insurance. Tarantino had never known his father, Tony Tarantino, a deadbeat dad who'd bailed on Connie and her infant son. "I never knew my father," Tarantino later said in a 1993 *Daily Telegraph* interview. "He was never part of my life. I didn't know him." The childhood absence of Tarantino's biological father hurt him tremendously. That pain stayed with Tarantino as an adult, evidenced by his ultimately severing ties with biographer Jami Bernard after she interviewed his father.

JAMI BERNARD: I'd tried to track down Quentin's father for my book [*Quentin Tarantino: The Man and His Movies*]. I tried very hard to track him down, but I couldn't find him. And I discussed this with Quentin. You know, Quentin loved my book. We sat down and had dinner in Toronto and I discussed this at length. I told him about all the attempts I had made to track down his biological father, and he didn't have any real comment about it at the time. I know it would have been a big deal for him if his father had been found, but he didn't think it was wrong of me to try to find as many people to talk about him as possible.

But the thing is, the father found me after the book came out. He contacted me by e-mail and offered me an interview, so I figured if I ever updated the book, I could include that. So I interviewed him, and I printed it in *Premiere* magazine. Before I printed it, I went over all the facts of the story with Quentin's mother, Connie, to make sure this was the guy. Then I told his mother and publicist Bumble Ward to alert him to the fact that this was going to be running so he'd be prepared because I thought it might be an emotional shock. He had about two months to prepare himself. But then when the story came out, I guess it was too much for him to see a picture of this guy talking about him as though he knew him. Quentin got really upset over the article, and I'm sure he still holds it against me.

As is all too familiar a story when abandoned children grow up and become successful, Tarantino's father tried to reconnect with his now-famous adult son. After his attempts to reconcile were rebuffed, the elder Tarantino then exploited his son's fame to land lower-level jobs as an actor and director.

As a child, Tarantino had been quite close to his stepfather, Curt Zastoupil, who was a musician. Through Zastoupil, Tarantino had come into contact with lots of artistic people, who played music, wrote poetry, and created different kinds of art. This helped set Tarantino on an artistic path. He and his mother would often attend double and triple features at a local movie theater, often seeing films with more adult content than what most other kids were watching.

CONNIE ZASTOUPIL: We went to the movies all the time when Quentin was younger. I don't think I took him to see anything inappropriate, except for the time I accidentally took him to see *Deliverance* when he was a young kid. But I didn't know what the film was about. One time I took him to see *Carnal Knowledge*. During one scene Jack Nicholson kept telling Candace Bergen, "Come on, let's do it." And she said, "I don't wanna do it." "Come on, honey, let's do it." And Quentin piped up, "What does she wanna do, Mom?" And the entire theater erupted into laughter!

Zastoupil and the young Tarantino also practiced a number of "outrageous hobbies," such as fencing, archery, and even owning hunting falcons. Tarantino became an avid cineaste at a young age and also began reading comic books and Elmore Leonard crime novels. At the age of fifteen, he was arrested for stealing a paperback copy of Leonard's *The Switch* from K-Mart. The author's work would later inform much of Tarantino's writing. Not only is Leonard's influence visible in both *Pulp Fiction* and *True Romance*, which he once described as being "very much an Elmore Leonard novel kind of story," he would also adapt the author's *Rum Punch* for his 1997 film *Jackie Brown*. (It might be noted that both *The Switch* and *Rum Punch* feature the same characters.) For a time, Tarantino and his *True Romance* collaborator Tony Scott would toy with the idea of adapting *Killshot* together, with Scott directing Tarantino and Robert De Niro. Tarantino also considered adapting the Leonard-penned western *Forty Lashes Less One* with Samuel L. Jackson, but neither project materialized.

CRAIG HAMANN: Here is another area where I have to credit Quentin. He's the one who turned me on to Elmore Leonard. He also turned me on to Donald Goines. That's an author I had never heard of before Quentin. I had no idea who he was. Those kind of books—the pulpish kind of books—just walk hand in hand with the kinds of films we were watching and the kinds of things we were interested in. Even Asian cinema. I know it may seem like, well, what do guys like Donald Goines and Elmore Leonard have to do with Asian cinema? Just the fact that they were stepping across the line, those creative boundaries, and were doing more than what other people were doing. At that time in Hollywood, things were getting kind of repressed and restricted, and there were these rules about how the bad guy had to be depicted and what things could happen on screen. But with things like Donald Goines, Elmore Leonard, and the Asian movies, that wasn't the case. Same thing with the Italian spaghetti westerns. They had anti-heroes and characters who were deeply flawed that were the protagonists of the stories. Those things really influenced both of us. Quentin's movies have always been influenced by those things.

Years later, when I made my own film *Boogie Boy*, there is a scene where Marc Dacascos is talking to Jaimz Woolvett. They're talking about back when they were in prison and Jaimz Woolvett is asking Marc's character about what was going on there. And Marc's character talks about someone had gotten killed, and how he was a cool guy who had turned him on to all these Donald Goines books. I just put that in there because that's what Quentin had done for me.

Tarantino was, by most reports, a bit of a mess during this period. He could be rambunctious at times and somewhat trying even for his closest friends.

RICHARD "RICK" SQUERI: He would be calling for rides at two or three in the morning. All of that was just part of Quentin. And you accepted that if you were going to call yourself his friend. That was part of his charm and also part of the pain in the ass he was. I knew his mother Connie, and she was a wonderful lady and a single mom. I kind of think she didn't know what to do with a teenage boy at the time, because his hygiene was a little questionable. We would get the word from other people in the class to "tell your friend to take a shower." The kid was trying to work several shifts at the Pussycat Theater. He was all over the place. Your heart would go out to him, and it was kind of obvious that he didn't have a good male role model. There were several common-sense things about life and survival that he didn't know about, but then he had this wonderful enthusiasm for film.

I remember my future wife and I took him to the premiere of Arnold Schwarzenegger's first *Conan* film [*Conan the Barbarian*]. That was at Twentieth Century, downtown. So we went and saw it and we realized when we were talking about it afterwards that he really had a different take on it. He didn't really understand the difference between love and the relationship in it. Amidst the kind of primitive violence that was in it, there were a couple of points there where you got to see that the character is human and that he cares about other people. That kind of thing just didn't enter his mind at all. We kind of started to figure out between us that that was a piece that hadn't really made it into young Quentin's mindset yet. He had an incredible mind for the shot and for film and for the action, but not that.

Hamann took an interest in his younger friend, showering him with praise and support. In many ways, Hamann was instrumental in Tarantino's maturation, even going so far as to teach him to write. "He didn't just teach him how to compose, he literally taught him how to write," explains Squeri. "He could scribble, but there was no way you could read anything. It wasn't legible."

CONNIE ZASTOUPIL: I've always been very fond of Craig. I liked him right away, and we're still friends today. He was older than Quentin, but I thought that might be a good, stabilizing, mature influence. And it turned out they were very much in tune with one another age-wise.

At the time Tarantino and Hamann were attending the James Best Acting Center, Hamann was sharing a house with a buddy named Todd Henschell. Hamann and Henschell had known each other since attending Eastern Michigan University together in the mid-1980s. Hamann had come to Los Angeles first, and Henschell later followed. Their college film instructor had asked his students to sign an agreement stating they would assist one another when and if they made their way to Hollywood. "We all agreed that if we knew someone else from our class who was already out here, we would team up or try to help one another," recalls Henschell. When Henschell first relocated to California, he discovered Hamann living in a rundown place called Equestrian Inn. "We used to call it Cockroach Inn," laments Henschell, recalling an insect infestation problem.

Citing the exorbitant cost of living in Los Angeles, the two friends decided to rent a house together in Burbank, not far from the airport. As planes were constantly flying over the house, it was often difficult to hear one another without shouting. "The sound of the planes was driving Todd crazy," Hamann recalls. "He was damn near ready to start shooting at them. We could hardly hear ourselves think." (It should be noted that a line about living next to the airport later found its way into Tarantino's script for *True Romance*.)

When Hamann first introduced them, Henschell wasn't sure what to make of Tarantino. The two would ultimately become friends, largely on the strength of their both having extensive video collections, but Henschell's first impression of Tarantino wasn't all that great.

TODD HENSCHELL (set photographer): I thought Quentin was a knucklehead. I thought he was a screwball, because he had, I believe the polite phrase is, an abundance of personality. At least that was the Quentin then. I don't really know him now. But I came to realize that we liked so many of the same things for the same reasons, that it was really hard not to like him. If you have a lot of that stuff in common, that's sort of a bonding thing. So we had that right away.

He turned me on to directors I had never really thought about. I ended up becoming a big John Carpenter fan because of him. He helped me to realize how sophisticated John Carpenter's directorial skills were.

But if you experienced Quentin in large doses, he could be overly taxing because he was enthusiastic like a puppy. It could be too much. It was like, dial it back. He was very loud. If you took him out in public you were like, "You've got to cool down, dude." And that's not a criticism, he was just very excitable. But at that time, if you could peel back that sort of bombastic part of him, he was a real film historian. Anybody who studies their craft, whether you go to college or just study a lot of movies, you have to respect that. That is, to me, the highest thing you can do—study and master a craft.

In 1982, Tarantino went to work as a clerk at Video Archives, a cool little Manhattan Beach mom-and-pop-style video store. The store was co-owned by Lance Lawson and brothers Rick and Dennis Humbert, who also served as managers. Lawson had previously co-owned a video store in Redondo Beach called Video Outtakes. When he and co-owner Dean McGill had a disagreement and ultimately parted ways, Lawson brought his share of the Video Outtakes inventory to the new store. Lawson and the Humberts' first hires were two former Outtakes employees. These were Dean McGill's son

Scott and Roger Avary, who was "kind of a founder" (Avary), adding to the store's inventory by supplying Atari 2600 and Intellivision games for rental. Avary wore many hats at the store, even writing the database for the customer tracking program on an Atari 800 computer.

ROGER AVARY (producer, coworker): I first met Quentin when he was a customer at Video Outtakes, and it was on my recommendation that we hired him at Video Archives. Rick didn't like Quentin. He said he smelled bad and he said he couldn't write very well. If you've seen Quentin's writing, you know he had messy handwriting. But there are other reasons to hire someone beyond their proficiency for penmanship.

On Avary's recommendation, Lawson spoke with Tarantino and was impressed with his knowledge of film and filmmakers like Brian De Palma and Sergio Leone. Based on these things, Lawson took a liking to Tarantino and hired him. According to Lawson, a selling point for Tarantino was his being granted permission to sign out as many free videos as he liked.

Tarantino would later tell author Paul A. Woods (*The King of Pulp: The Wild World of Quentin Tarantino*): "The only thing I could do was get a job at this video store because of my knowledge of movies. And it ended up being like my college, all right? It's not that I learned so much about movies when I was there—they hired me because I was, you know, a movie geek—but it stopped me from having to work for a living, basically. I could just work at this place and talk about movies all day long and recommend movies all day long."

ROGER AVARY: I later worked on the screenplay for a movie called *Lords of Dogtown*, which David Fincher was going to direct at the time. It's a completely different film as it exists now, but the reason I worked on that was the sense of connection I felt toward the Zephyr Surf Shop, because it felt very similar to Video Archives. The video store was like the surf shop; if that was the thing you were into, you gravitated there to be around other like-minded people in the pre-Internet time. You gravitated toward this one common location where everyone there loves the same thing that you loved. I modeled the depiction of Skip Engblom, the person Heath Ledger wound up playing, after Lance Lawson.

Video Archives would become known for its extensive selection of cult films, classics, and foreign offerings, ranging from French New Wave to Shaw Brothers kung fu epics. These types of films attracted a certain type of employee who loved movies and knew all about them. Tarantino best personified this. Tarantino knew anything and everything a person could possibly want to know about cinema. "I always prided myself on my knowledge of cinema knowledge—who directed what, who starred in it," Lawson told author Jeff Dawson in *Quentin Tarantino: The Cinema of Cool*, "but Quentin knew all of that plus all the details—the supporting cast, who wrote the screenplay..."

Adam Groves, a frequent customer of the video store, would later recount his experiences in the store in this excerpt from his eulogy "RIP Video Archives," which appeared on the now-defunct *Fright Site* website.

> *Video Archives, which started in the early eighties, as a hole-in-the-wall located at 1822 Sepulveda, was indeed the greatest video store in the world. Now I'll grant that all such distinctions are subjective and subject to the whims of memory and nostalgia, particularly in this case, as the business in question has been closed for over nine years. I've patronized a number of video stores since VA's closing that may possibly be better ... but was unable to make a first-hand comparison in any case, so Video Archives remains at the top of my list.*
>
> *I remember this now-famous establishment vividly: my family, after all, was, according to an overheard comment by one of VA's longtime clerks, "there since day one." I even recall my customer number: 387.*
>
> *At a time when video rentals were a novelty and most video stores had puny selections, Video Archives had everything: Hollywood blockbusters, documentaries, foreign films (organized by country, an unheard-of innovation at the time), cult flicks (which had*

their own wall, another innovation) and the all-important "adults only" section. The place also had a cool big-screen TV, where I experienced my first taste of quite a few great films. An added attraction was the guy who worked there whom we knew as The Tall Guy with the Big Chin. You know him as Quentin Tarantino.

You're aware, I'm sure, that the one-and-only Quentin Tarantino worked as a video store clerk prior to hitting it big...well, Video Archives is where he worked. As I remember, he was always amped, plugging any given video with such enthusiasm you felt you had no choice but to rent the damn thing. I specifically remember Tarantino selling my mom on Unfaithfully Yours *and myself on a James Bond flick (it might have been* Diamonds Are Forever*). After watching the videos, we both agreed it was more fun hearing Quint talk about 'em!*

Linda Kaye, a friend who first met Tarantino as a Video Archives customer in search of Mickey Rourke films, was immediately impressed by Tarantino's now well-documented encyclopedic knowledge of film. But then everyone who met him was.

LINDA KAYE (actress): He had a memory that was amazing. He could watch the credits and practically tell you who the wardrobe mistress's second assistant was on some obscure little 1982 indie film. It was just astounding. Sometimes, just for amusement, we would ask him weird stuff like who stunt coordinated a certain movie. And he'd know. He'd always know.

RICHARD "RICK" SQUERI: Quentin had a tremendous memory. I actually left parts of the business because I don't have that kind of memory. I could really just look in awe at people like Quentin who have that kind of memory and that kind of recall. That's really helpful. If you can look at a hundred films and cut them together in your head into another film, that's incredible.

ALAN SANBORN (actor, production assistant): Everyone always talks about Quentin's vast knowledge of movies, and that is certainly true. But what a lot of people don't realize is that he has an equally impressive knowledge of songs and music. He knows all of that stuff. He can tell you what song any given group did at what time. He has an encyclopedic knowledge about pop music. Something that really impressed me was, we had a Christmas caroling party one time—we were just singing Christmas carols in the house—and Quentin knew so many Christmas songs. I think I know most Christmas songs, but Quentin was the only person I've met who knew everything I knew and then more rare and obscure things that I didn't. He just knew all of them! That isn't necessarily what you think of when you think about Quentin Tarantino.

I remember we used to get into these bets all the time about this song or that song and then having to look it up to see who was right. Invariably, it was always Quentin who was right!

RUSSELL VOSSLER (coworker): Quentin was then as he is now, full of energy and full of knowledge.

"I kind of fancied myself the Pauline Kael of the store," Tarantino would later tell author Paul A. Woods. "People would come in and I would kind of hold court with them. Eventually—and this was great for the first three years, and a major drag the last two years—people would come in and just say, 'What do I want to see today, Quentin?' And I'd walk them through it: 'Well, this is *Straight Time*, it's with Dustin Hoffman, it's one of the greatest crime movies ever made,' and so on."

The employees at Video Archives would ultimately become a close-knit group of friends. They all shared a love of film, and at least three of them—Tarantino, Roger Avary, and Scott McGill—had ambitions of becoming film directors themselves. Tarantino and Avary eventually became Oscar-winning screenwriters and directors in Hollywood. Most everyone who knew or worked with McGill says he was also extraordinarily talented.

CRAIG HAMANN: Scott was the kind of guy who, if you knew him, you would have paid money to see the world through his eyes for an hour or two. He was very eccentric, in a good way. He was very unique and had a great sense of humor, although it could be kind of odd at times. He was charming. I loved Scott. I thought he was one of the coolest guys around. He was a little quiet...not that he didn't talk or anything like that, but he was very soft-spoken. He never screamed or yelled or anything like that. He was a good friend to all of us, the kind of person you looked forward to seeing. He was very talented, too. He made some really great Super-8 movies. He was the type of guy that, while you were working with him, he would do a camera angle or move the camera in a way that, in the back of your mind you would ask, "What the hell is he doing?" And then you'd see the movie and you'd say, "Oh, that really looks cool!"

McGill and Avary, who were such close friends that everyone likened them to brothers, collaborated on a "wild, wild" horror screenplay called *Pure Hell*, which they never filmed. "There was almost no plot," Hamann recalls. "On every single page there were all kinds of crazy dark things happening."

Unlike Tarantino, Avary, and Hamann, success wasn't in the cards for McGill, who ended up taking his own life in 1987.

Two other employees, Russell Vossler and Gerald "Jerry" Martinez, were more interested in becoming artists than they were filmmakers. (Russell and Jerry, a sketch artist and a painter respectively, as well as Jerry's brother, Steve, had actually met at the El Camino College Art Department in 1980.) Other members of the gang included Stevo Polyi and Rowland Wafford. Although they weren't Video Archives employees, Linda Kaye and Steve Martinez also hung out with the group.

STEVE MARTINEZ (friend): My brother Jerry was working with Quentin. I remember that Quentin would come over to the house. He'd always pick up Jerry and they'd watch a movie. But he would never come in. He'd always be outside with the car running and Jerry would run outside to meet him, so he was sort of a shadowy figure. This was in 1983, maybe '84, and I finally met him. I'd go into the video store to see Jerry, and then I got to know Quentin. I saw right away he had a great sense of humor. He was a very funny guy and I tried to impress my own humor upon him to see what he thought of it. I guess he liked it, because we became friends, too. I never worked at the video store, but we saw plenty of each other.

Under Lance Lawson's supervision, the video store was a fun place with a light atmosphere. Things were a little stricter when the Humberts were in charge, but it was still a relatively light atmosphere. "Until I became a director it was the best job I ever had," Tarantino would later say.

RUSSELL VOSSLER: Video Archives had kind of a record store vibe, probably because several of the employees had worked previously in record stores. It was really, really relaxed and freewheeling. This is what it was like... Jerry Martinez, who was a close friend at the time, worked there, and he introduced me to Rick Humbert. This was in 1984. This is how I remember my job interview with Rick:

JERRY: This is Russ. He wants to work here.

RICK: Okay, you're hired.

The video store became a sort of clubhouse where members of the group hung out for fun. There was a big-screen television and chairs in the center of the store, and the friends would show up even when they weren't working to screen movies. The group frequently held "movie nights" there. Tarantino enjoyed introducing his friends to films they weren't aware of, so he would often select the films that were shown. He would stand beside the television and enthusiastically introduce the movies, sharing anecdotes and bits of trivia about their history and production.

Tarantino was extremely serious about these movie nights. On one occasion he banned Steve Martinez for being "a jackass" (Russell Vossler) because he didn't believe he was taking *Red River* seriously enough. Apparently, Martinez was talking during the screening and making jokes. In another instance, the two locked horns over *American Ninja*, which was a Tarantino fave. On yet another occasion, they clashed over the merits of the Sylvester Stallone actioner *Cobra*, leading to Tarantino storming off angrily, declaring, "*This is something I take very seriously!*"

In her 1995 biography, *Quentin Tarantino: The Man and His Movies*, Jami Bernard detailed a heated argument between Tarantino and Steve's brother Jerry, which took place the first time they met:

> *Jerry had been to a sneak preview of the Joe Dante film Gremlins and hated it. Quentin, who loved Dante's frequent allusions to comics, Warner Bros. cartoons, and Famous Monsters magazine, loved it.* "Part of the Video Archives scene was you got together and talked about movies," says Jerry. "So I finally meet this guy everyone says I should meet and he argues with me. Maybe I was being a little bit of a snob, a little judgmental about films at that time. That's one thing I really learned from Quentin is that all of these films have a value, there isn't one that should be more important than another one if it's true to itself. You could make some little mindless comedy, but if it comes from a pure place then it's every bit as valid as *Gandhi*.

A similar thing happened to Russell Vossler just after meeting Tarantino, who was giving him a lift home in his Honda Civic. During that ride, Vossler made the mistake of professing his love for Alfred Hitchcock movies, which got under Tarantino's skin. Soon Vossler found himself in the middle of an argument he didn't want or expect. "I didn't even really know him and we were already having a big argument," recalls Vossler. Tarantino was a huge Brian De Palma fan, and his contention was that De Palma's work was superior to that of Hitchcock.

RUSSELL VOSSLER: Jerry and I were big Hitchcock fans. I was more interested in art than I was movies, but Hitchcock was a passion for me. Anytime the theater in Santa Monica would have a retrospective, I would beg and borrow and cajole people to go to these screenings with me. And Quentin didn't care about Hitchcock back then. I don't think he does even today. He preferred De Palma, even though De Palma was very much influenced by Hitchcock. So we would always debate the merits of those directors.

STEVE MARTINEZ: He had some funny arguments. He would stick to his guns, but I think when you're wrong, you're wrong. And

I don't know if he was just being contrary or just trying to be overly cool by being so outrageous, but he would have these opinions like *Psycho 2* was better than the original *Psycho*. He thought *Rocky II* was superior to the first *Rocky*. Really outrageous. Especially the *Psycho* argument. Psycho is considered a classic. I'm not a movie guy, but I think that's the general consensus. But if you listened to him long enough, he would almost start to make sense. He had some wild opinions. I almost doubt he really believed some of them. He may have been just saying that to be saying it. He was very staunch in his opinions.

Jerry came in there and he was a big Alfred Hitchcock fan. And I think Quentin got him and exposed him to other things—stuff like the French New Wave. Quentin was a huge Brian De Palma fan.... He loved *Body Double*. He would say these things were superior to Hitchcock's films. Even though they were sort of homages or remakes of Hitchcock, they were nonetheless superior. Things like that would sort of rankle our nerves.

LINDA KAYE: There were some films that Quentin thought were overrated and some he thought were terribly underrated.

CRAIG HAMANN: Quentin and I agreed on most movies, so there wasn't much need for us to have many debates. I do remember that he really disliked *Star Trek III: The Search for Spock*. I liked it, so we had a pretty good debate about that. He felt the movie gave lip service to doing all these great things, but didn't really do it. I started pointing out the things it did do, and we sort of went back and forth.

Although the atmosphere of Video Archives was laid back and was somewhat of a clubhouse at times, Russell Vossler stresses that it wasn't all fun and games. "I know a writer's job is to 'print the legend,' as they say, because the intention is to sell books, but Video Archives was first and foremost a job in those days. I don't think we should over-mythologize it. It was a cool job, don't get me wrong. Looking back through rose-tinted nostalgia, it might have been my favorite job. But it was low pay and no future. It was a job-type job, as Quentin later wrote in *Reservoir Dogs*. But with a slight amount of freedom."

That freedom included employees having the ability to take money out of the register whenever they got hungry and craved pizza or Mexican food. "We were just asked to write it down on a sheet so they could keep track of it," recalls Vossler. "That of course ended pretty quickly, because we weren't making a lot of money. So that would result in x amount of dollars disappearing out of the till for food."

Members of the Archives group also hung out together after hours away from their "job-type job," which closed its doors at 10 p.m. When they did, their focus was still on movies.

DENNIS HUMBERT: You had four or five guys working a shift who were all good friends. When the store closed, they usually all went out to a movie together or went and hung out somewhere. They were all best friends who shared a love of movies. They got along really well. All of them dreamed of making it in the movie business. It was a pretty happy atmosphere.

LINDA KAYE: We all, as a group, used to go out pretty regularly. We would all go down to Westwood as a group. You know, one or two carloads of us; maybe six or eight of us. And that would be Stevo Polyi, Quentin, me, Russell, Roger, Rowland Wafford, and then the occasional girlfriend. We all would go to see whatever movie had just come out and was hot that Friday night. Quentin was just so much fun to take with us. He was just so entertaining.

We'd all be standing in line at the theater, just kind of looking at our money, standing in line, and he'd say, "Hey you guys, wouldn't it be cool if, all of sudden, right now, somebody just, like, walked right up to us…and killed us? Just, like, blasted us with machine guns. Wouldn't that be cool?" And we all just kind of looked at each other like, "Yeah, that'd be cool." And he was like, "Just think. Wouldn't that be weird? Just so random, you know?" And we were all trying to understand how a thing like that could be cool.

I think his definition of cool meant, you know, if it were a scene in a movie—not if it really happened. I said, "God, Quentin. If that really happened then we'd all be dead and that would be really sad." And he'd still be like, "Yeah, but it'd be cool." He defended it. He completely defended it. He'd say little random things like that that would just make us all look at each other. It was then that we knew why we took him with us. Where else are you gonna get entertainment like that? Certainly not in the theater. And that was just one of a jillion things he would say.

When Tarantino's friends from this period reflect back, they all comment on his insatiable appetite for film. He absolutely loved movies and was unabashedly obsessed with them.

STEVE MARTINEZ: Quentin was very enthusiastic and I believe that's part of his success. I think that if you spent time with him, even way back then, you'd walk away with a real high because he was very positive. He really lifts you up, and I think he brings that to his films. I think when he works with people, he tries to create a really positive atmosphere. He was just a really enthusiastic guy. Sometimes he would drive me a little bit nuts, though, because it was always just the one subject: movies. I used to give him a hard time about that.

CRAIG HAMANN: Quentin watched a lot of movies, but he had a reason for doing that. He did it because he wanted to be a filmmaker. He told me, "If I had to have heart surgery, I would want a doctor who was up to date on everything; a guy who was completely up on his craft and has studied every aspect of it. I don't want a doctor who says he studied a few things and didn't need to study anything new." He said, "If a person wants to be an expert on something, to really know how to do it right, he has to absolutely know his craft." And that's what he was doing when he watched all of those movies. And he was one hundred percent correct about that. He was patient and he watched everything he could get his hands on.

STEVE MARTINEZ: I remember once we were all hanging out over at Jerry's apartment and Quentin was taking a nap. Then he woke up, and this was like nine or so. The first words out of Quentin's mouth were, "Let's go see a movie." I thought that was pretty funny. And again, I would always give him a hard time about that, but he was single-minded and he knew what he wanted to do.

It was pretty much non-stop, to the point of obsession. He wasn't afraid to let anyone know what he knew. He got us all interested in Sonny Chiba, and we would all get together on the weekend to watch *Shadow Warriors*. He was usually the first one to know about these things, and quite often, his tastes were correct. So we became Sonny Chiba fans and we'd meet every weekend and we'd trade places. Everybody would take a turn hosting it on Sunday night. Again, that was his idea. And you know, he really loved those blaxploitation movies.

DENNIS HUMBERT: For Quentin, it wasn't at all unusual to watch five or six movies in a single night. He'd work until ten or eleven and we had this thirty-five-inch Mitsubishi big-screen TV, which was pretty rare at that time. We had that there in the store and Quentin would watch movies all night. We'd wake him up at nine or ten in the morning and he'd be asleep on the floor. He'd just get up and start working again. His enthusiasm for film is what I remember.

RUSSELL VOSSLER: I forgot about that. Yeah, he used to sleep in the store sometimes. We all had keys, so it was no big deal. I think Quentin used to sleep back in the hall that led to the restroom. That was the store's adult section. He camped out back there because that area wasn't visible from the front door.

When the Video Archives group hung out together, they would observe traits and interests in Tarantino that would later rear their heads in his screenwriting.

STEVE MARTINEZ: The scene from *Reservoir Dogs*, where they're talking and they're all arguing about the tip. You know that one? Maybe you already know this... Steve Buscemi is Mr. Pink and he's the one guy who doesn't want to leave a tip. Of course, Quentin plays one of the other guys trying to get him to tip the waitress and so on. Well, that was actually a case of art imitating life from when we would all go to Denny's or wherever. And Quentin was Mr. Pink—he wouldn't tip.

That was taken from real life. Then we'd all get into a big fight because he wouldn't tip. The arguments the character is giving are the real-life arguments we heard from Quentin. We'd all go out to have dinner together, and we all knew, "Okay, we're gonna have to put up with this after the meal when it comes time to pay." I thought that was pretty funny because the roles are reversed in the film.

RUSSELL VOSSLER: Quentin was kind of famous for that. He never tipped. He didn't believe in that kind of thing.

Another instance of a well-known Tarantino interest popping up in his work involves women's feet.

LINDA KAYE: He seems to like feet. Um, let me be delicate. [When I saw *Pulp Fiction*] I had to laugh because they were going on about this whole foot massage thing. And I'll admit it: Quentin's given me a few foot massages, but I think he's probably given them to lots of girls. It was really just a thing between friends. It wasn't... I don't mean to quote *Pulp Fiction*, but it didn't mean anything the way he made it sound in the movie. We were such good friends at that point that, you know, if Quentin had a sister, he would have rubbed her feet, too. And I'm not implying any incest, okay? Although I can't see him doing it for a guy friend, it seemed not inappropriate at the time.

STEVE MARTINEZ: He does love feet. He has a foot fetish. That's a definite sexual turn-on for him. Yeah, we all know about that. Like in *Jackie Brown*, when you see the close-up of Bridget Fonda's feet. I guess he'll just throw the feet in there wherever he sees fit.

As Quentin's screenplays would be completed or eventually made into films, his friends would often see things they had said in conversation later appear as movie dialogue. He would also use stories and scenarios suggested by things they had said in his work. This didn't offend anyone. Most of them were delighted to see their words immortalized this way.

STEVE MARTINEZ: [Quentin] was a very good listener. He just is. That's something he has. I don't think I'm a great listener, but like a lot of people, I just sort of wait my turn. He really listens and, as we all know, kind of soaks up information so he can use it again.

QUENTIN TARANTINO: That's what writers do. If someone tells you an interesting story, you remember it and you use it.

DENNIS HUMBERT: There were several parts in *Reservoir Dogs* that he used from the stories I told him. He even used some of the names. I created the name Nice Guy Eddie for a guy named Eddie Carpinski who used to hang around the store. He was just a really nice guy. And being from the car clubs, we pretty much nicknamed everyone with some kind of name. In another scene in *Reservoir Dogs*, the characters discuss a girl who Super-glued her husband's penis to his stomach...

QUENTIN TARANTINO: Dennis was a gambling guy at the Gardena casinos, so one of those dealers was kind of a badass guy named Fred McGarr. And Fred McGarr came down to the store and worked a couple of days and the three of us went out and had a drink. Fred McGarr told the story that's in *Reservoir Dogs* about the girl Krazy-gluing his dick to his belly.

Another case of art imitating life was an infamous line of dialogue that Tarantino says first in *My Best Friend's Birthday* and Christian Slater repeats later in *True Romance*: "I'd fuck Elvis." According to Humbert, Tarantino once told him that he'd fuck Elvis.

DENNIS HUMBERT: Quentin told me that seriously. He came up to me one day and he was serious. He looked at me dead seriously in the eye. We were watching *One Night with You* and Quentin came up to me and said, "Dennis, I'm not a fag. But if I had to do it with any man, I'd do it with Elvis." And I thought, what a thing to say! It was just so off the wall that it really cracked me up.

STEVE MARTINEZ: I think he may have said that. I don't know about that one specifically. Actually, I don't think that line was all that original. I heard it, but I think Burt Reynolds said something to that effect, only about Errol Flynn, in a movie once. So I don't know that that line was really that original.

Lance Lawson recounts a different story regarding the origin of the "I'd fuck Elvis" dialogue in *Quentin Tarantino: The Cinema of Cool*:

You know back then, Quentin was a bit of a homophobe... He really was a kid who'd never been out of LA county. Being able to travel the world was such a broadening experience and so good for him and that's what I'm happiest about—it really made him a better person. But you know, I'd kid him back in the old days, you know, 'Would you sleep with Elvis?' And the thought just kind of terrified him, and he'd go, 'No, no, no, no. I'd have to think about that,' and I'd go, 'Come on, this is Elvis... The King,' and he'd go, 'Would you?' and I'd go, 'Not necessarily Elvis, *but with Bowie maybe,' because I was really into David Bowie at the time. And he'd go, 'You would?'*

In the mid-'90s, several biographies of Quentin Tarantino were published. One story that was discussed frequently in those was a tale involving Tarantino becoming enraged and jumping over the counter and attacking a Video Archives customer. Roger Avary once detailed the incident, saying Tarantino "grabbed this guy by the back of his head and—*bam!*—slammed his head into the corner of the counter," adding that "blood just kind of dripped out of the guy's head into a pool in his eye socket."

STEVE MARTINEZ: I wasn't there to see it, but it happened. The guy was a pretty little guy, I think. I was a little bit unhappy with Quentin for deciding to pummel him because he was maybe a bit of a jerk, but... It's a little bit like his later shenanigans. He was getting into trouble there for a time. He likes to maybe be a little bit of a tough guy. I think he took that opportunity on a lesser opponent—unduly, I think—and battered him. But I wasn't there for it, and for what it's worth, I heard afterwards that Quentin felt really badly about it. I think it was as he was beating him, he was sort of like, "Why did you make me do this?" But I'm sure the guy, to some degree, had it coming. But yeah, it's a true story.

Quentin went over the counter and tackled him. He was whaling away on him. One time I arrived at the store and I went out to Quentin's car and took out his jacket. I was going to wear it as sort of a joke, but he came out of the store right at that moment. He didn't know it was me and he was ready to rumble. So yeah, that's a true story.

RUSSELL VOSSLER: Quentin and I almost fought one time. I know he kind of beat up a guy who was working there who was stealing from the store. I guess you could say he was kind of pugnacious then. He's not a short-fused guy, but he could get that way. You have to remember, he picked up a lot of things from the movies. I think he was inspired by movies a lot. That was my impression at least. When he and I almost fought, he kind of calmed down suddenly and apologized. I remember it feeling like a movie scene and not a real-life scene.

CRAIG HAMANN: Movies rubbed off on his behavior because that was his world, but I think Quentin was always Quentin. For anyone who is in a microcosm, and willingly there, they're going to be influenced by their surroundings. And he certainly was. You know, the things about him wearing the skinny ties and having the pompadour hair weren't so much movie things or even influenced by Elvis. Quentin really was a rockabilly boy. He was really into rockabilly music. He loved it, and I'm sure he still does. Both of us were dressed like that back then because we liked that type of stuff. But things that Quentin saw in the movies—and I was just as bad—probably did have an influence on the way he thought and the way he felt about things. But at the end of the day, he was still just Quentin. He had his signature on everything he did, even his personality.

RICHARD "RICK" SQUERI: Here's the thing about Quentin. In his mind, he would start off as William Smith, and then he would have to end up being Wally Cox after he'd started something. First of all, he was an absolute gelatin mass of a man. He hadn't had any training, and there was no form to his behavior at the time. It was terrible. When Craig or I were around, he sort of knew he had backup, so he would use that. He would just kind of get up in people's faces. He was a lot of bark and no bite. There was nothing there for a real bite. I don't know about the story where he attacked the guy at the video store, but he would have only been headed for embarrassment if it was someone with means or ability. But in his mind, he was William Smith. In his mind, he's not gonna take any shit. Unfortunately, that was not the case in reality.

With money occasionally missing from the till after a night of pizza and movies, and Tarantino physically attacking customers, things had a tendency to get out of hand at Video Archives. The employees were no doubt having a good time, but manager Dennis Humbert was less than pleased. He then felt it was his duty to act like more of a boss than Lawson, but, according to his employees, sometimes he crossed the line between tough boss and mad dictator.

RUSSELL VOSSLER: Dennis was much more of an authority-type boss than Lance was. Dennis was kind of an imperious figure at that time. He also managed card clubs, so he was kind of a tough, hardboiled guy. This is funny: one time he came in, and I think he was drunk, and he got really angry and fired everybody. I don't remember what exactly he was mad about, what set him off that night, but he was handing out firings. First, he fired Jerry. Then he fired Quentin. I was just standing there looking at him sort of aghast, and he said, "*What are you looking at? You're fired, too!*"

ROGER AVARY: Dennis had been drunk at the card club all day. Sometimes he would come by when we were working on a Saturday night and bring us prime rib and baked potatoes in Styrofoam. But on this night, he was drunk and violent, moving around the room like a prowling animal. If you got into his laser-light stare, then that laser light went on you. At one point he started throwing down some cards, basically forcing me to play him. Suddenly this guy was saying, "Let's do fifty bucks a hand." Very quickly I was about $600 in the hole. He started getting violent. Then he got mad and fired everybody. He did shit like that all the time.

RUSSELL VOSSLER: It's kind of funny in retrospect, but we were all very serious about it at the time. I remember we all got together and had a meeting next door at the laundromat. We were like, "What are we gonna do?" Somehow, we all got our jobs back. I don't remember what happened though. I think maybe the next day everything was just better again.

QUENTIN TARANTINO: It's not very memorable to me, because we all were all hired back in like a day! Dennis couldn't operate the store on his own. He was sort of pulling the leash a little bit. We kind of treated the place like we owned it, so this was him saying, "Look you little sonsofbitches, this is my store!"

Away from Video Archives, Tarantino and Hamann were getting closer to making their own films. Most of the key components were in place and the alliances had been formed that would lead to the creation of those. By this time, Tarantino and Hamann had both left the James Best Acting Theater. Hamann had begun attending the Van Mar Academy, which was run by Ivan Markota. Although Tarantino was not officially in the class, he would often tag along. It was there the two of them met and befriended an actress named Crystal Shaw. Shaw's career was on the rise. She had already done a number of soap operas and commercials. In addition to her acting, she also performed a variety of jobs like assisting with the casting for other people's films. One of those functions included casting Tarantino and Hamann for a voice-over in a comically re-dubbed German film à la *What's Up, Tiger Lily?*. The film was titled *Sex Olympics* and featured Tarantino voicing a character known only as the Oracle.

CRYSTAL SHAW (actress): I was working as casting on a couple of small films. One was a martial arts film called *Sword of Heaven*. And shortly thereafter I asked a bunch of fellow actors from class to be in the movie for scenes I was casting, so we kind of just put each other in stuff. I was really trying to figure it all out, and I was really young. I was managing this crowd scene of actors. Quentin and Craig were there as I had invited everybody from my acting class. There was a group of people I had hired who were punk rockers. At the time, they looked pretty scary, although kids today dress that way to go to school. They had nose rings, torn clothes, tattoos, black eye make-up, and earrings and colorful hair. They were mostly teens/early twenties, but they were really acting very tough.

So I had this scene where I was supposed to rally and I said, "*Yo, Statue of Liberty, get over here!*" Quentin pulled me aside and said, "Crystal, you just went up against a six-two actor who was intense and scary and you said, 'Yo, Statue of Liberty!'" He started laughing so hard. What I loved about Quentin was that things tickled him. I love his laugh and making him laugh. He observed life. He observed every detail. I saw that and made note even at that time. I said, "This guy observes a lot of stuff." I thought, "He should be an actor. He would be amazing."

Quentin started inviting me to go and talk acting. He would invite me to go to this little restaurant called Lamplighter on Lankershim, deep in the valley. It was a little rundown diner. I loved it because it was so old fashioned. I would go there in my '80s dress with my huge cobalt blue purse, and Quentin would be in a black suit. We might as well have been in the '50s. We were having coffee and sandwiches. And he started talking about film and this scene and that scene. He would even say things like, "You know when you said that line?" He would remember a line of dialogue I had done a month before. "That reminds me of this film when this actor did this..." I said to myself, "This guy is a genius." This was before we really knew anything about geniuses or how the brain works. He and I could rival one another for who talks the fastest, but Quentin would probably win. Plus, he had an overabundance of film history and information. If you've spoken to him or seen him in interviews, that's how he was. That was not an act. That was Quentin, and he usually had that level of energy. He has a wealth of information. He notices things. He pays attention. If you watch the backgrounds of his scenes, I guarantee you he either set up or approved every little detail in the background. Some directors notice this stuff, and others don't. He just impressed me. I knew he was gifted right off the bat. He just saw things so much differently, I knew he was either brilliant or a dreamer. Apparently, he's both.

Quentin and I had endless conversations, mostly about movies. He would treat me to lunch, which I appreciated. He would say, "Can I buy you a sandwich?" And we would talk endlessly, mostly about movies. I remember him telling me to watch the movie *Blow Out*. He wanted me to see it. He was telling me about the Nancy Allen character and why she was intriguing and why the audience loved her. He was very complimentary about her, saying she looked like she was from the Midwest, but she had this other side to her.

Quentin was really impressed with John Travolta's talent. He thought he did such a great acting job in *Blow Out*. He used to talk about Travolta this and Travolta that and how he was an underrated actor. "People don't understand how brilliant John Travolta is." He would get so animated. Quentin just adored Elvis, and I always thought Travolta had that vibe, so it made sense. I told him, "You don't have to convince me about John Travolta. I'm in love with him." He was gorgeous and charismatic, and really did a great job and was versatile. He was also one of the first male bimbos I think we ever saw on screen, right? In *Welcome Back, Kotter*. Anyway, when Quentin later cast him in *Pulp Fiction*, it was surreal. It was amazing. I was sitting at home watching the news and they were talking about Mr. Tarantino's next film will be starring John Travolta! I just flipped out! Who would have ever thought that would happen?

In the early to mid-'80s, I was getting offered all these flirty, sexy roles which were becoming largely in demand at the time. There was a deluge of bikini and horror movies. Theatre only pays so much rent, so I was like, okay, I'll do a few of these goofy movies. When talking with Quentin about it he would say, "Just be yourself. Don't try to act sexy. You already are just by being yourself. When directors call you in for a sexy role that's because they already think you have the appeal that they are looking for." Such great advice. It even helped me get a part in *Hardbodies* as Candy, a character who actually does put on acts to try to be sexy, just because she wants for people to like her. So that advice worked for a natural appeal, or a put on one for certain roles.

By the mid-'80s, most of the key alliances had been formed and the pieces were in place that would eventually lead to the creation of *My Best Friend's Birthday*. But before Tarantino and friends could make that movie, which they would all refer to as their personal film school, they would first attend a sort of preparatory school. This would be a small film (even smaller than *My Best Friend's Birthday*) called *Warzone*, which would be directed by a guy named Al Harrell. This is significant because Harrell would later assist them with My Best Friend's Birthday, and also because it would give them the tools and the know-how to eventually move forward and attempt to make their own film.

PART TWO

INTRODUCTION
THIS IS MY ON-SET STORY, TELL ME YOURS
by Jason Pankoke

"Archaeology is the search for fact ... [W]e cannot afford to take mythology at face value."

— Dr. Henry Jones,
Indiana Jones and the Last Crusade

Most of us have not played a major hand in a full-length motion picture from beginning to end on any budget level. We've thought it. We've dreamed about it. We've entertained plans to put a story before camera at some point in the future. For many, that future might have passed ten, twenty, thirty years ago already. It's okay. We won't judge. It takes a special level of mettle to muscle through even one of them, from the creators to craftspeople and everyone else involved.

What you might *not* want to admit is you have ephemera tucked away from your blaze of filmmaking glory that didn't quite pan out. The Super-8 or 16-millimeter film footage never transferred. The consumer-grade videotapes not unpacked or played in ages. The completed micro-epics that simply can't hold a candle to your present-day professional work or even the comparatively sophisticated films made by today's young people. The keepsakes from the sets of other productions not your own. They remain as a sort of dowsing rod that can lead back to your movie past at any time.

Only if you want to go there, of course. Memories are the most valuable and vulnerable collateral left regarding those projects boxed up in the closet, attic, or basement. You may not easily recall every single thing about your valiant movie efforts, yet the sensations and learning moments linger:

Leave day job early. Take token nap. Hit late lunch quick. Arrive on set. Check in with producer and director. Watch others show up. Watch others take their place on set before you. Wait. Wander among crew on fringes. Wait more. Return to staging area. Zone out. Snap to it when producer calls your name. Punch code in keypad so ticket prints out in kitchen. Repeat. Again. Return to staging area when cinematographer says the shot is good for camera. Wait. Take notes for future remembrance. Small talk with other actors and crew waiting in wings. Watch awesome new Beastie Boys video on near-silent television. Again. Check script. Wander back to set. Take photographs during scene rehearsal. Return to staging area. Yawn. Snap to it when producer asks you to drive an actress home. Return to set. Wait. Stand in to hold boom in cramped office scene. Return to staging area. Glaze over. Notice sun rays seeping through window blinds. Wait for wrap to be called. Pack up and leave when wrap called. Go home and sleep. Zzzzzzz. Repeat willingly.

Twenty years later, this description is a composite of my first experience participating on a film set as best as I can remember. It's not very exciting on paper, I know. Despite being a bit older than the crew as well as a full-time employee elsewhere, I gave in to my curiosity. Why not call the number on the flier? My inexperience in all the roles I played—gofer, set photographer, boom operator, and late-night voice of reason – was not a deterrent in their eyes. Thank goodness! Students filled all the key positions one would expect on a larger and professional show, carrying over what they were learning to do through class work in Chicago, and it proved invaluable to my understanding of what filmmaking looks like.

It's too bad I've never seen it. Was it ever finished? The director planned it as her thesis project, so it must have been turned in for the grade before her graduation. Online information reveals that she has moved on to other forms of media including journalism and viral marketing for a living while this film receives no mention anywhere. All is said and done here, probably. That's okay. It served the purpose for the folks who needed it. At the least, I have my prints, contact sheets, notes, and shooting script to help me imagine what the finished product may have resembled.

Not all films need to be profusely accounted for and preserved. Collectively, we don't have the lifetimes or resources to do so. At the same time, numerous low-budget pictures exist in the world that deserve to be known by a readership and found by an audience. I first put this theory into practice with *Micro-Film*, a self-published journal dedicated to the contemporary indie cinema. Over its seven-year run, I wrote about dozens of movies and watched many dozens more—from prestige narratives and documentaries released by the top non-Hollywood studios, to desktop wonders made by backyard impresarios with their friends and families. Micro-Film rolled with the tide caused by the "Indiewood" wave of the '90s, the fabled theatrical release of *The Blair Witch Project* in 1999, and the entrance of affordable digital production tools into the consumer marketplace.

My heart always lies with the true underdogs and idiosyncratic voices in the scene. My soul realized during the *Micro-Film* era that media creators all have stories to tell behind the stories they actually told on screen. Therefore, my mind had to root through the evidence in order to select the ones that had the most potential for good editorial. This included a conscious decision to incorporate just enough tales of highs and lows to give readers a more realistic expectation of what the act of filmmaking entails. Occasionally, interview subjects told me or my writers about projects that did not make it past the planning, financing, or post-production stages. One can only imagine the exponential heartbreak of a film, *any* film, progressing far enough and then becoming mired in limbo, unfinished and unseen.

That is and isn't the case with *My Best Friend's Birthday*, the "lost" feature conceived by screenwriter Craig Hamann and directed by co-writer/co-star/video store clerk Quentin Tarantino. Never completed or formally distributed, the rowdy comedy of errors can only be found in remote corners of the Internet as a VHS bootleg-quality compilation of various scenes and a pockmarked shooting script facsimile. Tarantino fans have known of it and still debate over whether it should be included in his formal filmography. If it's not, so what? This late '80s relic shot on the sly in Los Angeles with a skeleton crew and the tightest of $5,000 budgets *is* his first significant film effort any way you slice it, although its reasons for being should be squarely credited to Hamann, and hovers over the famous filmmaker's *oeuvre* like a shimmering specter in a pompadour. It is stylish in context but dated in reference, static in framing yet dynamic in dialogue choices and character quirks, more intriguing by far than the little student film that went nowhere due to the generous amount of patented Tarantino tics on display. This effort directly points towards bigger cinematic things to come.

For now, the persistent myth that has shrouded *My Best Friend's Birthday* from clear view will be demystified to a degree as this book's interviewees continue discussion. They address how an earlier incomplete production called *Warzone* led them down the *Birthday* path, why this project came about, what happened on a set populated mostly by neophytes, and where they feel it resides in the grand scheme. As more than one person will remind the reader, this fascinating fragment served as an unofficial film school for them all. Many of us may even relate to their anecdotes. Therein lies the worth of revisiting this very notable micro-film, a continued promise that any of us could still strike it big after starting small.

— JASON PANKOKE is the editor and publisher of the regional film "local 'zine" *C-U Confidential* and the programmer of the annual New Art Film Festival. He lives in Champaign, Ill., and has been a professional book designer and illustrator for more than 20 years.

MAKING MOVIES

Although Craig Hamann wasn't a part of the Video Archives group, he and Tarantino were practically joined at the hip. They would talk about movies ad nauseum and would attend screenings of old movies at the Hollywood Theatre revival house at 6764 Hollywood Boulevard. According to Sharon Waxman's book *Rebels on the Backlot*, a representative double feature was the pairing of the Jack Nicholson film *The Border* and a cannibal flick called *Dr. Butcher, M.D.*

Tarantino and Hamann worked on some no-budget homegrown movies during this period, collaborating with other would-be filmmaker friends. One such pal was a guy named Al Harrell. Hamann's roommate Todd Henschell had first met Harrell while the two were working at a temp job indexing documents. "Everyone was kind of afraid of him," says Henschell. "But I walked up and said, 'How are you doing?'"

TODD HENSCHELL: I got Al right away. I could tell he was a smart guy. I said, "What are you doing here? You don't look like you belong here." And he said, "What do you mean?" I said, "Well, I don't belong here, and neither do you. But we need money, right?" We started talking and found out we loved a lot of the same movies. So I invited him over to watch some movies and he said okay. He was like Quentin—he was kind of a film historian. We had conversations about our favorite directors of photography and individual scenes we liked, going back to [*Citizen Kane* DP] Greg Toland. Those are the kind of discussions you really enjoy.

Hamann agrees that Harrell was similar to Tarantino. "I can remember Quentin and I talking about Al Harrell," Hamann says.

"We both determined that when Al writes or directs something, it doesn't really matter if it's good or bad, because Al will put his own unique take on it and make it interesting. I think Quentin is that way, too. Quentin always has a vision, which is very important when making movies. Also, like Quentin, Al had seen a lot of offbeat indie movies."

Harrell would ultimately succumb to cancer many years later in 2004. True to every known description of Harrell, he remained tough until the very end and never complained about his illness.

CRAIG HAMANN: Al Harrell was a very good friend of ours. He was from Philadelphia. He moved to Los Angeles to write and direct. He was black, so it didn't take him very long to learn that it was going to be a harder road for him because of his skin color. The industry was and is very biased. He started doing low-budget indie movies. Some of those were pretty damned good.

TODD HENSCHELL: Al was an amazing fellow. I wish he was still around. He was very gentle and very kind. But when you looked at him, he looked dangerous. He just had that look, like Ving Rhames, when he's pissed off. He was just a big, strong martial artist from Philly. He was very well educated and had a masters in theatre arts. We talked a lot. I was never a stage guy; I was a movie guy. But he was another guy we would say, "What about this scene in this movie," and he would say, "Oh, yeah!" Whenever you both have that in common, there's an immediate connection.

We had some great adventures together. One time he was going to show me Errol Flynn's abandoned mansion in Hollywood, except he got the map coordinates wrong. We ended up walking about twenty-four miles around town, trying to find the street. And we couldn't figure out where it was. That was the Bataan Death March for me. I remember thinking, I can't take another step! I couldn't pick up my legs. And he said, "It's just around the next corner!" I said, "Al, you might be built like a cyborg Terminator, but I can't do it anymore! My feet feel like they're the size of pumpkins!" But he was a very tough, never say "give up" kind of guy.

Preparing to shoot a scene involving Clifford (Al Harrell). (Courtesy of Todd Henschell)

QUENTIN TARANTINO: Al Harrell was the greatest guy. He was a very interesting fellow. He lived hand to mouth the entire time I knew him. He lived in this boarding house on Hollywood Boulevard in what was then one of the worst parts of Hollywood, right across the street from Playboy Liquor. It was one of those boarding houses with the toilet down the hall. He was always leaving his stuff in storage or leaving his stuff at someone's house because he couldn't keep it. He would have a gym membership just so he could take showers. He never really had any money, but he had enough money to go to the movies every once in a while. We went to the movies all the fucking time. He was one of my best friends during my twenties. We saw so many movies together, and we would talk on the phone for like three fucking hours.

TODD HENSCHELL: He had a heart of gold. I would never say anything bad about him except for this: sometimes I think he had some screwy ideas. You know how sometimes you get those mailings from banks saying, "If you open an account with us now, we'll give you $500"? And it's just $500 worth of credit, right? They're not really going to give you $500 because then the bank would be out of business tomorrow because everyone would go down there.

I said, "They're not going to give you $500, Al." He said, "Well, that's what it says." I told him to go down to the bank and ask them for five one hundred-dollar bills when he opened his account with twelve bucks and see if he'd get it. So, he had those screwy thoughts sometimes, but if you were in a jam, he was your guy. If you needed to move furniture, he would do it. I called him and said, "We're moving." And he said, "I'll help. Just tell me when you need me."

CRAIG HAMANN: He was trying to get a movie called *The Judas Contract*, which had a pretty good script, off the ground. He wrote and directed a teaser for *The Judas Contract*, which Quentin and I worked on. That was a lot of fun. But Al ended up getting ill. In the beginning it was diabetes, and then later he found out he had cancer. And he wound up passing away without getting the opportunity to do the things he wanted to do with his life. He was very talented, and just a genuinely nice person. He was also a martial artist, so we used to work out together a lot. And he was great at weapons fighting. He used to teach me how to use things like a staff or sword, which I didn't know at the time.

QUENTIN TARANTINO: I eventually lost contact with Al, but I never meant to. I never really wanted that, but at some point, I started distancing myself from him just a little bit. Something started happening to him... It was the thing that happens to a lot of people who work at something for a long time, and then it never happens. He got bitter. Everything started having a bitter tone, and everything was something negative; he was negative about the movies, and he was negative about this, and he was negative about that. I was just allergic to that kind of negativity because the only thing that was keeping me going at that time was positivity and encouragement based on nothing. I didn't need a Debbie Downer, telling me how it really is. So I slightly distanced myself from him, and then my life went in a different arc, so I never saw him after I started making movies. I just completely lost touch with him.

Oddly enough, I still own an entire script that Al wrote in pencil. I have that among my writings. He wrote it and left it at my house one time, and he never got around to getting it back. And I never threw it out, I still have it. And it was a neat idea, too. It was my favorite of his writings. It was about a serial killer who kills people by poisoning them. He would go to a bar and meet a girl, and then he'd poison her. Then as he was talking to her, the poison started working he would tell her she was dying and what the symptoms were going to be. And then he would walk away and she'd die five minutes later. It's a pretty fucking good story.

During this period, Tarantino was working on a number of scripts himself, hoping one of them might sell and get his foot into Hollywood. Tarantino wrote out his treatments and screenplays by hand. He would then hand over his scrawled notebook pages to Craig Hamann and Linda Kaye, who would provide feedback, show him encouragement, and type the scripts up into proper screenplay format.

CRAIG HAMANN: Quentin would give me some scenes written in pencil on notebook paper, and I would type it up for him. I'd correct grammatical mistakes and clean it up, but other than *My Best Friend's Birthday* and *The Criminal Mind*, I don't recall us working on any other project together. I did, however, type up his screenplays for him sometimes. Plus, we used to sit together and cold read scenes from his screenplays; kind of act them out just to hear them.

One thing that I did do was help Quentin with his writing style. The first pages he gave to me to type up on *True Romance* are a good example. Back then it was called *The Open Road*. And in that screenplay, the lead character, Clarence, was writing a screenplay called *Natural Born Killers* as he was going through his own adventures.

Anyway, the first pages weren't that good. Not to say that Quentin's writing wasn't good, but he was hurting himself by overwriting. Hell, it took all day for him just to set up a scene. I told Quentin to trim everything. In fact, I said to Quentin, "With your writing all anyone's going to care about is what are the characters doing, and what will they have to say about it?" Quentin came back a few days later with new pages that were very much like his lean and mean style we now see. Don't get me wrong, I did not create Quentin's style; I just helped him find it within his own work. It was already there. He deserves credit for the talent part, that's for sure.

LINDA KAYE: I remember one thing Quentin came up with that I thought was just brilliant, and I don't remember hearing this anywhere else. Quentin and I were talking about a scene for some early film that he wanted to do and didn't have the budget for. He said, "There's a girl on a bed talking to a guy and she needs to brutally murder him. Hack him to pieces." And he goes, "I just don't have the budget for those kinds of effects." Then he said, "So, here's my plan." He proceeded to tell me. I believe there was some music playing in the background like, you know how an old-fashioned record player gets to the end of the record and goes *Kachunk! Kachunk! Kachunk!* Then the needle lifts up, goes back to the beginning of the record and sits down and plays the record again, right? Well, at the end of the music there was that silence when the needle went to the end of the record. During that time, you could hear dialogue. The conversation was becoming heated, and their voices were escalating. Then you see the needle go to the beginning of the record. And then he said he would slowly pan around the room, doing a complete three-sixty, starting at the bed and going around the room, around, around, around, just showing all the little crap on the wall—the little trinkets on the dusty shelves, the moonlight streaming through the slits in the blinds. The music is still going, so you can't hear anything. When the camera comes all the way around again, you see her sitting on the bed, bathed in blood.

I said, "Quentin, that's brilliant. That's fantastic. That way you avoid having to show the thing. Oh, my God. It's inspired. It's Hitchcockian." I was just going on and on because I thought so much of it. And it's funny how a low budget will force you into creative solutions that actually, even with a huge budget, you'd be wise to go with anyway. I don't think I need to keep selling it. It speaks for itself. You don't need to see somebody getting hacked to pieces, but you can see the aftermath. And you can't hear it because of this record playing. Everything is implied.

Then, the next time you see it, and you're seeing this three-sixty, you know what's happening. You know this guy's being hacked to pieces.

In 1982, Tarantino and Hamann collaborated with Al Harrell on a video film he directed called *Warzone*. Although it wouldn't be directed by Tarantino, he, like everyone else involved, learned a great deal about filmmaking during its production. This project would teach the crew members enough to prepare them for *My Best Friend's Birthday*, which would ultimately prepare a number of them for careers as professional filmmakers.

The screenplay for the (approximately) $2,000 *Assault on Precinct 13*-inspired film was a collaborative effort written by Harrell, Hamann, and Henschell. Hamann describes the plot as such: "It involved three prisoners, played by Quentin, Rick Squeri, and myself, who are in a stockade at a secret U.S. biological warfare facility. A biological war takes place, and the prisoners don't even know it. They manage to escape the stockade and go out and find some people who are still alive. Little by little, the prisoners figure out what's going on. They double cross each other. Finally, there's a violent showdown at the end."

Hamann and Henschell's house in Burbank was disguised in such a way that it became many of the film's locations. In one instance, their backyard was used for a scene that was supposed to take place in a park. "Our landlord certainly didn't know we were shooting a video there," says Henschell. "But it was L.A. That stuff was happening all the time."

The shoot would prove to be a difficult one, especially given its minuscule budget. Its cast would consist primarily of acting students who were studying under James Best and Ivan Markota, who was another teacher Hamann studied under. ("The best thing Ivan did as a coach was get an actor used to the business game," recalls Hamann. "I learned what casting directors were looking for and why it was important to present myself a certain way during interviews.") The filmmakers stole locations, shooting without permits. Henschell would buy much of the equipment used on the film, and as owner of the camera, he would serve as Director of Photography. In addition, Henschell was also de facto script supervisor. "There was never a continuity person on any of these projects," says Henschell. "So I did that. I developed a good eye for that. I would tell people, 'You need to move over about a foot. That's where you were standing last time.'"

As would be the case with *My Best Friend's Birthday*, *Warzone* would never be completed, mostly due to economic factors. "The cost was just too much for us, especially trying to shoot it on video," says Henschell. "But we wanted to do something. Every weekend we would shoot a little bit of it if everyone was available."

CRAIG HAMANN: *Warzone* was a lot like *My Best Friend's Birthday*. We shot that with no money to speak of. Al, Todd, and I wrote a script, and we got some friends who were actors together. Quentin was one of them. He played the chief bad guy. I played his right-hand man. Our friend Rick Squeri played another bad guy.

QUENTIN TARANTINO: You know who my character was? The closest you would get to seeing what I did in *Warzone* was the McKenas Cole villain character in *Alias*. He was very similar to my villain leader character in *Warzone*, although he did it better. But you know, I was a jokey bad guy.

TODD HENSCHELL: Craig was a villain, too, but he was a villain who turns into a hero, very similar to events in *Assault on Precinct 13*. Rick Squeri, who's a great guy, played another villain.

RICHARD "RICK" SQUERI: Craig, Quentin, and myself worked on almost everything together. We were a triple threat. We were kind of our own little film company, so of course we all worked together on *Warzone*.

TODD HENSCHELL: In the first ten pages of the script, the three "heroes" of the piece break out of a military detention compound and discover that all is not right with the world. And by break out I mean just walk out, because everybody else there but them is already dead. Or what passes for dead in this story... Think John Carpenter's *Assault on Precinct 13* tossed into a blender with *The Walking Dead*.

Here is an excerpt of representative dialogue from *Warzone* featuring the three characters, Rush (Hamann), Moungey (Squeri), and Needle (Tarantino). Henschell explains that the dialogue of the film was more technical and "expository clearinghouses" than grand theater. "This isn't a Tarantino script talking about Big Macs in Paris, you know?"

RUSH: That oughtta fix it, Mangy.

MOUNGEY: Don't call me that.

RUSH: What? Mangy? You're right. Asshole has a much better ring.

NEEDLE (to both of them): Shut up.

Needle moves to the control panel, which is hanging from the wall by the wires. He presses some buttons. Nothing works.

NEEDLE: The bastards playin' with our heads or what?

RUSH: If they wanted to do that, they could've just cut the power to the panels.

NEEDLE: That means this whole fuckin' place might be on emergency power.

RUSH: Sure looks like it.

Needle tries the door. It's still locked.

MOUNGEY: What're they doin', Needle?

NEEDLE: How the hell should I know?

RUSH: Who knows, Mangy? Maybe it's a test to see how long you'd go before doing something stupid. But then the test would already be over.

Craig Hamann and Rick Squeri pose for a photo after shooting a fight a fight scene in *Warzone*. (Courtesy of Todd Henschell)

MOUNGEY: I said don't call me that.

NEEDLE: Will you two back off? I don't wanna deal with your shit right now.

CRYSTAL SHAW: In the early '80s I was doing some days on soap operas, helping cast films, and was in an acting class with Craig. Quentin would sometimes come along. Craig and I worked together and we admired each other's work. Then one day he said, "There's this friend of mine who sometimes comes to class here and we're doing a movie, and he wants you to be in it, too. He wanted me to ask you to be a lead. It's called *Warzone*. I'm also going to be in it. Do you want to be in it?" I read the script and it was really good. So I met with Quentin for coffee, and course I said yes, as long as my schedule was considered.

"There was no going down to the store and renting a grip package for us," says Henschell. "We didn't have any money for that. Basically, any of the stuff you see on the set of a professional movie... We didn't have any of that stuff."

Because of this, Henschell fashioned some of the equipment himself. "I've always been sort of a troubleshooter/fabricator." When Harrell decided he needed a dolly, the filmmakers were astounded by how much a dolly cost to rent. None of the would-be filmmakers had enough credit remaining on their credit cards to even pay the deposit. So Henschell studied dollies and concluded that he could reproduce one himself. He used the steel box chassis from a photocopier, obtained some go-kart wheels, and drew up blueprints. He then took them to a welder, asking him to fabricate parts to attach the wheels to. Henschell created his own steering system, utilizing a joystick for controlling the dolly. "It was very compact and tight with big, soft rubber wheels," remembers Henschell. The filmmakers found the resulting dolly to be quite effective, and it would be used again on *My Best Friend's Birthday*.

Henschell also purchased the equipment and made his own lights, saving them money. When the crew would shoot entire weekends, they would typically spend around $50 on energy due to the lights. "Todd worked his butt off on *Warzone*," recalls Hamann. "He wore most of the hats and was constantly busy."

CRYSTAL SHAW: Al Harrell was very kind. I hadn't met him before, but when I met him, I just found him to be so kind. That's the thing I remember the most about him—his kindness. He was so gentle. When you showed up on set, he would be very kind, like, "How are you doing today?" Then he would say, "Here's what we're going to do today..." He was very explanatory and very calming. He kept everything moving and he kept everything level. He made you feel very comfortable as an actor. I really liked him and I thought, "This guy is a pretty good director." He didn't have a high energy level, which also has its benefits. Quentin would make suggestions, and it didn't bother Al. He would put his hand on his chin and nod, going, "Uh-huh..." With some directors that could have been a blow-up, but with Al it was not. Quentin and Al had a good collaborative relationship. All of those guys did. They seemed comfortable together.

Both Al Harrell and Quentin knew enough, even at that young age, to listen to other people and pay attention to suggestions that might help them to become better directors. They were both ego-less. It was like, "Let's make the film as good as possible, and let's have conversations about this scene and what we're doing here." And that's what the best directors do—they take in information that comes to them.

Al did a pretty good job. Al had studied the script and he had studied the sides for what we were shooting that day. He knew what he was doing, and he never got offended. He seemed more mature at that time, which is unusual for someone as young as he was. He was very generous, and that was rare.

TODD HENSCHELL: There's a funny part with Quentin in *Warzone*. We were shooting a scene where somebody stabs Quentin's character. It's his death scene. We shot that in the kitchen of the house we were renting. In the scene, a character had a knife they had gotten out of the cupboard and they jab him in the gut with it. They do a disembowelment strike. The shot we wanted was to see Quentin's face as he got stabbed, and then we were gonna cut to a low shot as he goes down on both knees with his legs folded behind him. *Thunk!* And then he falls over almost like a Warner Bros. cartoon character.

But Quentin couldn't get the falling to his knees and the falling over right. He had to do eight or nine takes. I looked at his knees and said, "You're gonna have to have surgery, dude." They were black and blue, even though we had put padding down for him. He said, "I want to get this right." I said, "You can't do this anymore. You're going to hurt your knees." But he refused to give up. When you're shooting video, one of the nice things is that it's cheap. We had lots of tape, so we kept trying to get it right. There

Warzone filming headquarters in Craig Hamann and Todd Henschell's backyard. (Courtesy of Todd Henschell)

were like ten or twelve takes. And he was a big guy. Every time he went down, he would strike both knees hard. Every time he did that I would grimace. But he refused to give up. I admired that.

CRAIG HAMANN: Quentin may have been suffering in pain, but he gutted it out to get his performance right. We were crowded in the kitchen and Quentin was being stabbed by Crystal's character. At first, he was falling back into a kitchen table chair, which got basically ruined. Then he was just taking the fall. He kept doing it until he got it right.

QUENTIN TARANTINO: I think it was my character's death

Tarantino's character Needle holding a .41 Ruger Blackhawk on John Bennett's General Garvin in the "nice night" scene from *Warzone*. (Courtesy of Todd Henschell)

scene. I think it was that my character got shot and I had to fall down. But I was giving it my all... Of course, I was giving it my all... We were having a ball. I vaguely remember that scene, and had forgotten it until you mentioned it just now, but I appreciate that people have a nice memory of me doing that.

CRAIG HAMANN: In my opinion, Quentin's performance was the best one in *Warzone*. He played a role called Needle. He was absolutely fabulous. It just rubs me wrong; I still don't think he's really had the chance to just dig into a role and show what he can do as an actor. The problem is that he's so famous that they just end up having him play Quentin onscreen. But back then he wasn't famous, and he put together a fantastic performance. It was funny, it was mean, it was scary, it was perfect.

TODD HENSCHELL: Quentin was very good at improvising, so there was a scene where we asked him to improvise. He had a library of crazy ideas he could pull up mentally anytime he wanted. The lights go off in the house and there's a dolly shot of an actor following this cable to find out if it's been cut. We come to the end of the cable and we pan up and see Quentin holding the plug. It's a very funny shot. He's got this huge .41 Magnum revolver that was actually Craig's. Quentin cocks it and basically points the barrel at the guy's nose and says, "It's a nice night if it don't rain."

It's hilarious and it's probably my favorite shot in the whole movie. But it was a bitch to shoot with our primitive dolly and no lights. I made a flashlight that had a car fog light in it and twelve-volt cable running up the guy's sleeve. By the end of the take the flashlight was trying to catch on fire. Because back then you needed a lot of light. They didn't sell the LED flashlight they have now that looks like the sun on a police helicopter. You couldn't get those then. So I had to build this high-intensity light and he was blowing on it to keep the smoke out of the camera. We made do with what we had. I think I got two takes out of that flashlight and then we had to quit because it was going to catch on fire in his hand.

CRAIG HAMANN: That line, "Be a nice night if it don't rain," was what Quentin's character Needle says to Colonel Garvin, who was played by John Bennett, when the bad guys take over. Quentin really made that role all his own. He never missed a beat playing Needle, who was a nasty but sometimes funny guy.

Warzone had its share of cool scenes, but as I said, we were really groping in the dark as filmmakers. But that's how a person learns. Many of the coolest moments happened when Quentin was in the scene. He had that effect on the movie.

CRYSTAL SHAW: I can't remember if I was blonde or light brown when we made *Warzone*; I used to go back and forth between blonde and brown and blonde and brown... But I remember Quentin insisting that I get a dark brown wig, and I thought that was so funny that it mattered. I remember there was a lot of talking between Al, Quentin, and Craig about my hair. So I went to the second-hand store and bought a brunette wig. That thing was sliding off me through half the shoot, but some photos did look good, but others not so much.

TODD HENSCHELL: We had fun. I don't think we ever produced anything that I would call watchable, and I'm the guy who shot most of it. I wouldn't want to watch it now, because I would look at it and say, "Oh my God, what was I thinking?" But it was a learning experience. Some people go to film school, and other people grab a camera and they just go make something. That's what we were doing. It was a great learning experience, and it was hard. You get into that weird fatigued psychotic state after you've shot for like twenty-eight hours. You're barely functional because your brain is so fatigued. But if I went back to that time I would do it again.

There was a lot of creativity there. When you're that age, you don't know what you can't do. By the time you get a bit older you become aware of the things you can't do, so you don't try them. But back then, we didn't know what we couldn't do, so we went ahead and did it anyway.

CRYSTAL SHAW: I remember there were many times when Quentin suggested different kinds of stuff to me. For instance, in one scene Craig was facing one way, and I was facing the other way. I had never been asked to do this in any film I had worked on prior to this one. I had been asked in theatre to do this strange "you look that way, and you look that way" thing where you looked at a focus point and you talked to the person. But doing that in film made me nervous. But Quentin said, "It looks great. You're gonna look great." It was very artistic, and very film noir. I can remember him trying to explain to me something like, "You've already been beat up, you may be dying, and this antidote can't be found. This creates tension."

And Craig was very serious in the scene because he knew the end of the film. But I didn't know what was going to happen, because I just got sides instead of the entire script. And I don't think they had the script fully completed yet. It was pretty confusing so I just had to trust the process, but it was tricky because I was used to doing plays where you know the whole story from beginning to end, so that kind of makes it easier to gauge things.

I remember I had a romantic scene with Craig. I remember Al coming over to me and wanting to talk to me. He told me, "Don't forget, this is actually intimate. You don't want anyone to hear." And then I remember Quentin gave me a couple more pointers suggesting to use my lower vocal register in this scene. And not to smile as much. Keep a straight face sometimes and just think about the scene. So every single person on the movie would give you advice to help you. It wasn't like they were bossing you around. I loved each of the little films we worked on and I always just took the attitude, this is going to be fun and at least you'll learn a little somethin' somethin', and it was, and I did.

I loved watching both Quentin and Craig act and create. It seemed like they knew so much. Sometimes when I was in scenes with them, I would get so wrapped up watching them that I would almost forget to say my own lines. Of course, every actor hopes they get to work with other good fellow actors, but those two were above and beyond back then.

TODD HENSCHELL: We made do with what we had. We stole shots. At one point we were shooting a scene with the bad guys in this movie. We were shooting this scene in an alley, and we were stealing it. We didn't have any lights or anything, and we were just going to do it really quickly. It was a shot with a bunch of people getting out of a van and running into the neighborhood. And apparently some neighbor thought we were breaking into the business we were behind, which we weren't, and we got stopped at gunpoint by the police. I was behind the camera and I remember hearing "*Freeze!*" I thought, "Who said that? That's not in the script." And then, Jesus, shotguns! Whoa!

CRAIG HAMANN: We all had weapons with us, which must have

**Craig Hamann dispatches a bad guy in a scene from *Warzone*.
(Courtesy of Todd Henschell)**

freaked out somebody living close to where we were shooting. All of a sudden, I saw police cars all around us. Because I was with Rick at the far end of the alley, we saw the police after Todd and Al did.

RICHARD "RICK" SQUERI: That really was one of the high points of our adventures together. We were going to go shoot in an alley near where Craig and Todd live. We go back there to shoot. We start to set up but we haven't done anything yet because we need electricity for the light and to recharge the battery for the camera. I've got a screw-in lightbulb socket that I keep because sometimes you can't get power anyplace. So you find a lightbulb, and you unscrew that, and you use that as an outlet. It's an outlet socket. We see that there's a light in the back of this small office building, but we see that there's a gate. So I scale the gate and jump down on the other side. Whenever it came to that kind of stuff in those days, that was me. That was my job—that was a stunt guy job. I get over, put the outlet in, and am just kind of getting set. I have my shotgun slung over my shoulder, and the rest of the guns are in the saddlebags on my motorcycle.

All of a sudden there's a cruiser creeping in at one end of the alley. I think they saw me hop down off the fence. Coming from the other side of the alley is another cruiser! There are at least four cops at the start, and the flashlight and the headlights are going. They tell us all to freeze. I'm supposed to drop my weapon. I take the thing off, sit it on the ground, and move away from it. Then they have us kneel down and lay down on the ground, interlacing our hands behind our heads. They're commanding us this whole time.

QUENTIN TARANTINO [To the author of this book]: It's so weird to hear you say "everybody's talking about this," like it's new, like it's news from the front or something! [Laughs.] You know, a story about something that happened when I was twenty-two! It's very bizarre! You know, "everybody talks about it..." But yeah, I remember when that happened. The cops showed up, of course, because we were fucking around in North Hollywood with guns and no permit in an alley behind some stores. [Laughs.] Of course, they show up for that!

CRYSTAL SHAW: I remember we were laying out there with all those guns and suddenly someone yelled, "*Get down!*" And I was lying there, face down, on the gravel in the alley and all these boots were all around us. I started giggling because I thought it was part of the scene! I thought it was a little bit overly dramatic, but I just went along with it. I don't remember which of them said it. "Please stop giggling! Please stop giggling!" And then Craig put his hand on my head to put my face down in the dirt and I looked at him like, what the...? And he had this extreme look of fear and I realized something was wrong. My face went farther into the ground. He said, not in a mean way, "Please be quiet, Crystal. It's for real."

And then these boots walked up next to us, and I remember all of the boots talking, and then Craig and Quentin talking, trying to talk their way out of it. There was some shouting. Al was getting yelled at. I had no idea why.

QUENTIN TARANTINO: The main thing I remember is what a good leader Al was. He says, "Everybody, this is all going to be great! I got you into this, I'll take care of it! Just hang tight, it's all gonna be okay! I got you into this, I'll get you out of it, just let me handle this!" That was cool. I really liked how Al stepped up as the writer/director into the leader position in that situation.

RICHARD "RICK" SQUERI: Al is trying to be in charge because he's the director. He says, "Don't worry, people. I got you into this, I'll get you out of this!" I go, "Hey Al, just simmer down. Be quiet." So the cops are saying, "Don't anybody move!" Al then says, "The object next to me on the ground is my glasses. I'm going to reach for my glasses." One of the cops says, "You do that and it'll be the last thing you ever do, buddy!"

CRYSTAL SHAW: That is absolutely true. At that point there were tears silently running down my face.

RICHARD "RICK" SQUERI: They came up and they picked up each one of us and we started to explain what the deal was. I said, "We're not doing anything. We're in a public alley. We haven't done anything. But I climbed over that fence." I think the guy whose office it was was in the cop car with them, because there was a civilian with them. He obviously lived nearby or above the store or something. We started talking about what we were doing. "Here's the camera. We've got these lights here. I was just plugging in so we could use the lights." There was no reason to hide it, because we were really trying to make art. I remember seeing the guy who must have been the owner of the store turn to the cops and say, "These are just kids. They must have been filming something." He no longer cared. He was just glad to find out we weren't cat burglars or whatever.

I said, "I'm sorry. None of these are loaded. I've got a plug in the barrel." They could see what was happening. I said, "To be clear, if you have to look, my saddlebag has other weapons in it." Then of course they wanted to see all the weapons, so we opened it up. I'm standing here with this cop, and we're casually appreciating arms together in this alley. I was an actor playing a holocaust biker, so I looked the part. So we're just talking guns now. The cops are fully appreciating what we have. They said, "Okay, you guys can't do this anymore."

CRAIG HAMANN: One officer took Todd to our house, holding a gun to Todd's head the entire time. It was ridiculous and overly-macho of the police officer. It made me angry, though I didn't show it.

TODD HENSCHELL: When the officer came inside, he saw the production board and all that stuff, and he knew what was going on. The cop remembered what town this was and says, "They're just stealing a shot."

But we did get a ticket for $250. We had looked into getting a permit to do one shot and it was going to cost us about $1,500. We didn't have that kind of money. We were taking this out of our food money.

CRYSTAL SHAW: When we got back to the house, another actress and I started crying. It was a scary situation. Everybody was scared. Especially Quentin, Al, and Craig who were all kind of macho guys, they were physically shaking. It was probably one of the scariest things I've ever encountered.

QUENTIN TARANTINO: We were all cool about it. We weren't scared. We weren't scared at all. It was just, we gotta let these cops know what's going on. A couple of the gals were scared, but none of the guys were scared. We knew it was gonna be fine.

Craig Hamann in a shot from *Warzone*. (Courtesy of Todd Henschell)

In addition to this incident, the filmmakers encountered other problems more germane to no-budget filmmaking.

CRAIG HAMANN: There were a lot of problems with shooting on video. That was at the time when people were just starting to shoot on video. When you watched it, the footage looked a little flat, but we tried to compensate for it the best we could. That was a nice project for Al to get his feet wet directing something.

TODD HENSCHELL: It never really got edited because, stupidly, we had thought, "This is tape, not film." With film you could go borrow somebody's flatbed and cut it and then give it back to them. But with videotape you can't do that. I had a friend who had an editing suite, and I cut some of it there. But I could only use that when he wasn't renting it. I cut some stuff. I cut a fight scene together. It was a cool scene and Rick did a great job setting up that fight. I think Craig actually hurt his neck during that scene, and he has that injury to this day.

But I could never get a bay to cut the rest of it. So it was never really properly cut. We just sort of did a video deck-to-video deck sort of rough assemble just to see what we had. I think the cheapest place I found was like $65 an hour. That's really cheap, even back then, but even that we couldn't do because we didn't have the money. In one hour, you can cut maybe one scene.

RICHARD "RICK" SQUERI: *Warzone* was a lot of fun. Unfortunately, it was directed and edited poorly, and it wasn't really the best script. But it was one of our very earliest efforts, and there were a lot of great things about it. We were all very, very young.

Eventually the filmmakers decided to shut down the production. "We all just moved on to other things because the inertia of the project had died down," says Henschell.

CRYSTAL SHAW: Al sent me such a beautiful letter months after shooting thanking me for my work. I thought that was super gracious. I still have that letter somewhere. Quentin also sent complimentary notes.

Hamann still likes the concept of *Warzone* and has since expanded the screenplay with the thought of maybe trying to remake the movie with a larger budget one day.

Hamann was a prolific writer during this period, producing numerous screenplays and treatments. One of these was a fantasy action script called *Thanotoid, The Last Quest*, which he and Squeri conceived during a hiking trip. "Craig was always writing," remembers Squeri. "He always had two or three projects in motion at any given time. And he would always tell me about these terrific characters he had written that I had inspired or that he'd written for me. That was wonderful." Squeri describes one such character as a doctor/priest/martial arts warrior. "It was a great part because he healed people, but he could kick ass when it was necessary," says Squeri. "That character was a lot more original in those days than it would be today. Those types of characters have appeared with more frequency since that time."

Hamann's other screenplays included multiple westerns and post-apocalyptic tales. "He would run these ideas by me to get my opinion," says Squeri. "I always enjoyed hearing about these things. They were all clever and original. They had both edge and heart, and that combination was something else that was not common in those days."

When Tarantino asked Hamann to write something for him to direct, Hamann wrote an eighteen-page treatment for a screwball comedy titled *My Best Friend's Birthday*. It was very much in the vein of Howard Hawks' *Bringing Up Baby*.

CRAIG HAMANN: Quentin and I started on *My Best Friend's Birthday* when Rick Squeri got married. They had a private ceremony, so we didn't attend that. But then they had their friends over for the reception, and Quentin and I had already been talking about making a movie. We didn't care that we didn't have any money, and we didn't care that we didn't know what we were doing. We had been watching a lot of movies, and we felt it was time to make one of our own. We had to come up with something, and I came up with this idea for a short film. I pitched it to Quentin during the reception. We were all fired up and drinking beers. He loved it. He said, "Write a script," and I did. It was only eighteen pages, but we expanded it to about thirty-five pages. And later on, when we decided we wanted to make a feature film, we added a lot of other stuff.

QUENTIN TARANTINO: At that time, I was really, really enamored with screwball comedies, where couples switch up, and I loved *What's Up Doc?* and *Bringing Up Baby*. I was really a big, big fan of Peter Bogdanovich at that time. My favorite movie of that era was his movie *They All Laughed*. Then I went and saw Alan Rudolph's *Choose Me*, which also had that same kind of comedic, romantic comedy roundelay, where characters match up and switch off. I just really liked that kind of movie back then, and *My Best Friend's Birthday* was my attempt to do that kind of thing.

Who contributed what to the final script has long been debated. Squeri recalls, "As far as I recognize and know, *My Best Friend's Birthday* was Craig's script that Quentin helped on. It wasn't really even a fifty/fifty thing."

Squeri sees many similarities between things Hamann first conceived with *My Best Friend's Birthday* and Tarantino's script for *True Romance*, which eventually sold for $200,000.

The screenplay for *My Best Friend's Birthday* is impressive. Despite being parts Hamann and Tarantino, there are a great many precursors to Tarantino's later work to be found in its pages, primarily its snappy and easily quotable dialogue, long-winded monologues, quirky characters and situations, and a plethora of pop culture references.

In reading the script (and viewing the existing scenes), it's evident that Tarantino and Hamann had many of the same influences and, in many ways, likely influenced one another. *My Best Friend's Birthday* will never be recognized as something on par with *Pulp Fiction*, but it clearly laid the groundwork for the films that would follow. It remains important in tracking the evolution of Tarantino as a writer and director, and is also significant because it served as a springboard to launch the careers of Tarantino, Hamann, and Roger Avary, who would all find varying levels of success in the film industry, writing and directing "proper" movies of their own. *My Best Friend's Birthday* also launched the career of Rand Vossler, the film's cinematographer who would later serve as a co-producer on *Natural Born Killers*.

CRAIG HAMANN: In *My Best Friend's Birthday*, the character Clarence was inadvertently getting Mickey into one mess after another. This is based loosely on QT's and my friendship. At that time, we were best friends. But Quentin could always find a way to mess things up for me. For example, Quentin had a habit of calling me late at night every time his car broke down, and no matter what kind of car he had, it always broke down. I'd have to go pick him up, and then he'd spend the night at my house. Well, I might have an acting audition or even a part on a TV show early the next morning, so I would need my sleep. But he'd call. I'd feel sorry for him and go pick him up. The next day I would be on the sound stage of some soap, where I was playing some role for a week, and I'd be half asleep. One time my car broke down on the way to pick him up after his car broke down. Things like that would always happen.

QUENTIN TARANTINO: Craig wasn't like his character Mickey and I wasn't like Clarence. Our dynamic was not that way. But we really were best friends, so the part where they really care about each other was accurate. We spent a lot of time together and were best friends. So our friendship was a jumping-off point, but they weren't really us. Mickey and Clarence were our acting alter-ego characters.

CRAIG HAMANN: One similarity we had to the characters, whether we knew it or not, was that Clarence and Mickey think they're the coolest guys going in their micro-cosmic world. Quentin and I had the same problem. We had all the answers, especially about what movies were good, bad, what actors were cool, and what actors had their heads up their butts.

TODD HENSCHELL: Craig and I shared an office and we were a couple of feet away from one another, so I knew about the project as they were coming up with it. Quentin would give him these scribbled notes on yellow legal pads, and Craig would turn that into a screenplay. He would say, "What do you think about this?" Craig and I cowrote several projects over the years, so we appreciated each other's opinions. We thought alike in a lot of ways. Our sensibilities were very similar. He would say, "Tell me if you think this is funny," and he would read me something. I wouldn't know if he wrote it or Quentin wrote it because I wasn't privy to that. But I would say, "That's pretty goddamn hilarious! I like that!"

I didn't know what was going to come of that, if that was something the two of them were writing to go do or whether they were going to try to sell it to someone. Gradually he let me know they were going to make it. I think it was when they borrowed a camera from [director] Fred Olen Ray, with whom I had worked with when I did props on *Star Slammer*.

Hamann secured an Auricon camera from B-movie legend Ray while working as an actor on his film *The Tomb*, starring Cameron Mitchell, John Carradine, and Sybil Danning. Through a chain of events no one seems to remember very well, Hamann convinced Ray to loan him his camera. Ray didn't think much about it, never giving it a second thought. He would only be reminded of it when Tarantino later credited him in an interview with the British Film Institute.

FRED OLEN RAY: If somebody hadn't come and told me I'd let them use my camera for their movie, I wouldn't even know it. I knew Craig from *The Tomb*, but I didn't really know him well. I'm not sure how they came to contact me. Somebody said later on they came down to the set of *Bad Girls from Mars* and watched us film that.

I had an Auricon, which was a sound-on-film camera. It was the old kind, with the big mouse ears, that used Mitchell magazines. It was the type of camera you could plug into the wall, and it had a toggle switch. That's all it had. You would turn that on and the camera would start running. But amazingly enough, it would run in sync with a Crystal-Sync Nagra. We used it to shoot a movie called *Evil Spawn* that we did with John Carradine. Then we loaned it to Craig and Quentin, and they used it on their movie.

I was surprised later on when I heard that my camera had been used to make the first Quentin Tarantino movie, but I had a vague memory of it happening. I just didn't remember the specifics as far as who those guys were. It didn't mean anything to me. None of us were famous at the time. If I had the camera today and someone I knew came up and asked to borrow it, I would loan it to them.

When they brought it back, I remember them saying they thought there were some kind of sync problems with the camera running from the wall current to the Nagra. I don't think that was really true, because it was used later by John Putch, who's a fairly well-known television director. He made a movie with that same Auricon camera. He used the camera and it worked fine for him. It was kind of an antique, but it did get the job done. It wasn't a great camera, but it was free. I was very quick to loan it to people. So if you didn't have any money, it worked great. That camera was sort of military-grade. It was a workhorse. Nothing could damage it.

TODD HENSCHELL: It was a loud camera. It didn't have non-synch. It was very hard to maintain sound synch. They were recording sound with a guy named Dov Schwarz. He was doing sound, but he could always hear the camera. So I built a blimp. It was really crude, but it helped. If the camera was reasonably close to the actor, you wouldn't hear that wrist watch ticking sound.

Tarantino and Rand Vossler working out a shot for the film. (Courtesy of Todd Henschell)

RAND VOSSLER (cinematographer): We built a sound buffer for it made of plastic sheeting and foam to help with the sound. The camera sound was audible a couple of times in our shoot, but we had a system in place for it. The camera only took 100-foot spools, so I was changing out the reels constantly. Each reel had two minutes and forty seconds, I think.

ROGER AVARY: I had access to an Eclair NPR 16mm, but the battery didn't work. So I studied the schematic and realized we could power it by connecting it to a car battery. So that's what we did. We couldn't even afford negative film. There was no money for any of that. There was the idea of, what if we used reversal film? What that means is when you edit, you have to be extremely careful because you're using positive film. There was kind of this attitude of "fuck it, let's do it."

TODD HENSCHELL: It was a time when I felt like almost anything was possible. That's a great feeling.

ROGER AVARY: Spike Lee's film *She's Gotta Have It* was an eye-opener for us. We suddenly realized that anyone could pick up a camera and make something without it having to be glossy and perfect. The idea was just, "Holy crap! We can make it with what we have," which was nothing. It was just the idea that there was no super-defined path. You just went out and did it. That was just becoming possible at that time, and *She's Gotta Have It* paved the way for all of that. It gave us a sense of freedom. It made us realize that you could make a black-and-white movie that didn't have expensive production value as long as you had a good script and good energy.

In addition to obtaining a camera from Ray, the would-be filmmakers also turned to another established filmmaker, Don Coscarelli, for advice. Tarantino and Avary had met Coscarelli through producer Roberto A. Quesada, for whom they'd worked together as production assistants on a Dolph Lundgren exercise video. (Quesada would also work for a single day as a cameraman on *My Best Friend's Birthday*.)

ROGER AVARY: Don was an incredible influence, along with John Carpenter, in regards to working on micro-budget films. He possesses a wealth of information on making low-budget films in Hollywood. We were just kids to him at that time. He gave us lots of good advice, and I applied as much of that to the film as I could. I was asking him, "How do I do this? How do I do that?"

One of the first challenges to making *My Best Friend's Birthday* would be finding an adequate cameraman. Video Archives coworker Scott McGill was Tarantino's first choice, but things became complicated when he met Russell Vossler's brother, Rand, in January 1985. Rand Vossler was a skilled cameraman in search of film work. At the time he was working a nine-to-five job as the manager of a Musicland record store.

RUSSELL VOSSLER: Rand had been a filmmaker for quite a while and had worked on quite a few things. He had gone to college for it at Los Angeles City College. He had a group of friends that he made films with. When Quentin and Craig started talking about making *My Best Friend's Birthday*, it seemed natural to get them together.

Scott McGill, the film's first cameraman (before later being replaced by Rand Vossler). (Courtesy of Todd Henschell)

RAND VOSSLER: Quentin wanted to do a short Super-8 film called *My Best Friend's Birthday*, and Russ encouraged him to get ahold of me because I'd been taking film classes. I had worked on probably thirty small films at that time; you know, 60mm student films and such. And he set up a meeting at Quentin's mother's house in Torrance and we sat down and met each other through *My Best Friend's Birthday*. At the time the screenplay was about forty-one pages. Quentin had dreams of doing it on Super-8 with some other friends of his—Scott McGill, who worked at Archives at that time, and Craig Hamann, whom Quentin knew through the James Best theater group. And we basically got together and read through the screenplay.

I loved Quentin's energy, and we just chatted each other up and I decided with much enthusiasm to encourage him to scrap the idea of Super-8 film and to lengthen the screenplay into feature-length form and shoot it as a 16mm feature outlaw. *Stranger Than Paradise* and *She's Gotta Have It* were two of such films that had come out directly prior to that. Quentin and I jumped on that right away. We were speaking the same language and basically started making the film together.

Scott McGill, who was a closer friend of Quentin's, had done probably four or five Super-8 films and actually had a great, great eye. I've said this before, but at that time, he was probably the most talented of all of us so far as having a distinct style. As a filmmaker, he just did everything himself; chopped the films, cut the films, scored the film's music, and just had a great sense of narrative that was lacking in most of the student films I was working on at that time. He was supposed to be the cinematographer, and I came onboard *My Best Friend's Birthday* after all of the basic plans had been laid and they had already done some casting on the film. The idea was that I would sort of help out and be a liaison for getting equipment and helping to set things up. Very quickly Quentin and I became partners creatively and Quentin never having shot anything didn't know anything about camera work and setting up the shots. Basically, with Quentin, everything [at that time] was just from being a film fan, but not necessarily knowing how things worked.

QUENTIN TARANTINO: I was financing *My Best Friend's Birthday* from a minimum wage job. Nobody came up with any money. There was no mom or dad or anyone putting up the money. I would raise up enough money until I had enough to

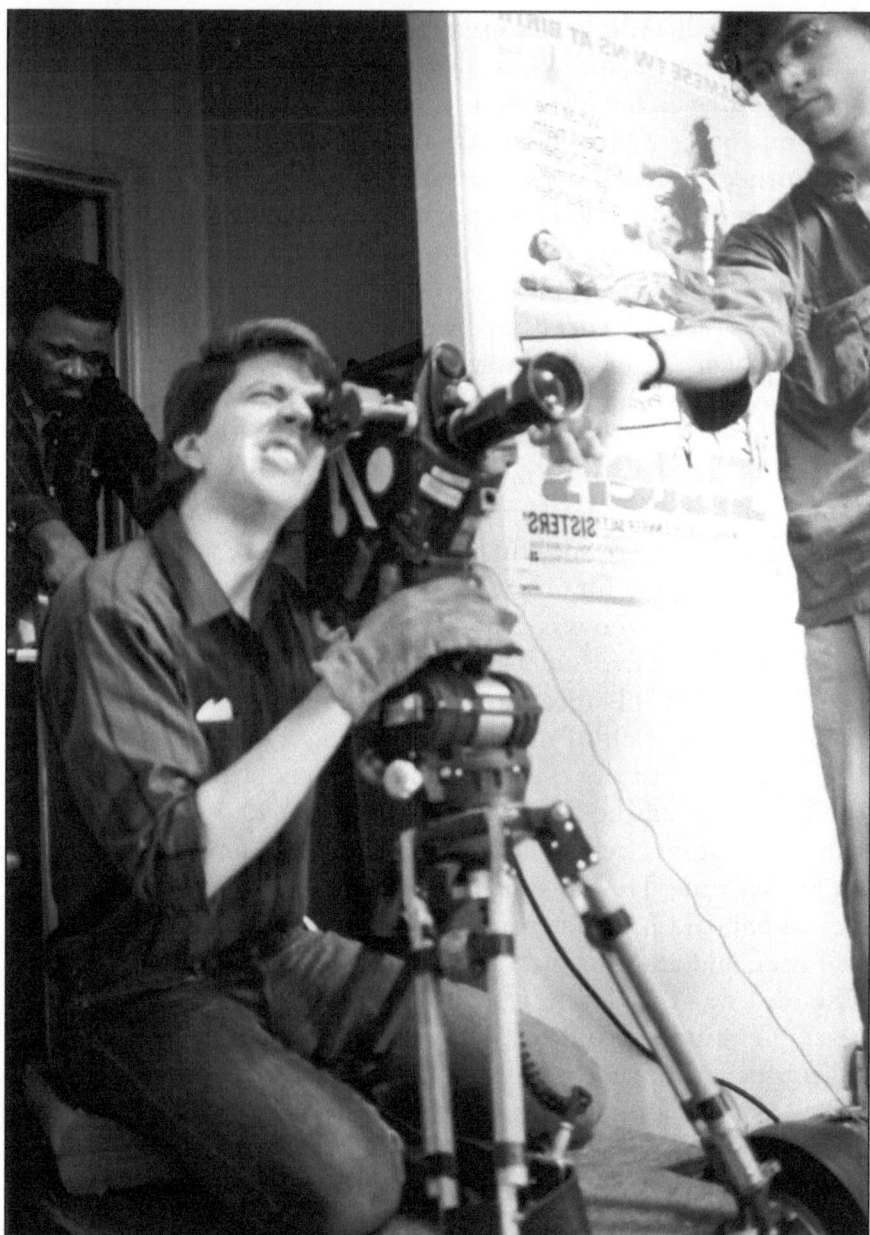

Cinematographer Rand Vossler shoots a scene. (Courtesy of Todd Henschell)

shoot for a weekend. And then either Scott McGill or Roger Avary would get the lighting package from either Arts Center or Cal Arts, where they went to film school. We'd get a package from them, and then if you rented equipment from Allen Gordon on a

Friday, you had it all weekend long for the price of a one-day rental. So I would just save up enough money that I could rent some lights, and maybe get a lighting package or a battery package, and then we'd shoot for that weekend. Then we wouldn't do anything for like two months, and then I'd have more money and we'd shoot for another weekend. We pretty much shot for like forty-four hours straight on those weekends.

RAND VOSSLER: Scott McGill was the cinematographer for the first three or four days and I was assisting him. We basically would set up the big shots and just so far as energy and pace, we needed to be working at about twice the clip we were working on. And it became pretty apparent, at least energy-wise, that something needed to change. Scott kind of stepped down and said, "Rand, you know what you're doing here. You should be shooting this film and I'll assist you." He basically became my assistant and I took over. Scott had never shot 16mm film and was kind of intimidated by the process, not that it's really much different at all.

CRAIG HAMANN: When we first started making *My Best Friend's Birthday*, Scott was our cinematographer. And Rand kind of took it away from him. Not because Rand was trying to be mean, but we were trying to get stuff done and Rand was more aggressive. But Scott continued to work with us on the film. He worked alongside Rand after that. Both Roger and Scott did a little bit of camera work on the movie, but mostly it was Rand.

RAND VOSSLER: After Scott and I switched roles and he began to assist me, he only stuck with the project for another week or two before he stopped showing up.

ALAN SANBORN (actor): Rand Vossler and I were part of a group of friends. A friend of mine named Bill Goodwin and I had entered Cinema II at Los Angeles City College at the same time. On the first night of class I was sitting there and I heard some people behind me talking about John Williams. I turned around and got into the conversation, and that was Dov Schwarz and King Wilder. The four of us became a clique. We were taking the class in the evening, and Rand was taking the same class during the day. So he kind of became the fifth member of our group and we would all help each other out with our films.

Sanborn, Schwarz, and Rand Vossler collaborated on numerous films before eventually working together on *My Best Friend's Birthday*. "I was in Rand's first movie, which was basically a technical kind of assignment," recalls Sanborn. "It was a series of different types of technical shots that had to be accomplished. But us being us, we made it into a story." The film had no title, but everyone involved with it would affectionately refer to it as *RVFF*, which stood for *Rand Vossler's First Film*. Years later Sanborn would make a "joking sequel" to the film titled *RVFF 2: A Film by Alan Sanborn*.

As the group continued working together, Sanborn began focusing primarily on acting and directing. Vossler worked mostly on cinematography and lights, and Schwarz worked as a sound technician. Other projects the three collaborated on during this period include the Sanborn-helmed films *My Brother's Keeper* and *Too Late*, featuring Vossler in the lead role.

It was during this time that Rand Vossler met Tarantino and Hamann. Vossler and Tarantino started hanging out together, and as a result, their cliques started crossing paths and working together. "It made sense to bring all these creative people together," Vossler recalls. At Vossler's suggestion, Sanborn cast Tarantino in a scene he was filming for a class.

ALAN SANBORN: I was taking a film directing class. We had to direct a scene in class one time, so I wrote my own scene. It was a little black comedy called *A Cozy Thanksgiving*. In the course of it there's this couple sitting down for their first Thanksgiving together, and then the wife's crazy family members start dropping in one by one uninvited. Each one gets worse than the last. Rand was playing the husband in that.

For some reason we didn't have anyone to play the last person who shows up, who's this crazy homicidal brother who's broken out of prison to come eat dinner with his family. So Quentin came into play. He came in last minute, as I recall. I think we had one good evening rehearsal with him in my mom's garage. Then we

Rand Vossler, Alan Sanborn, and Dov Schwartz hanging out with friends. (Courtesy of Alan Sanborn)

Rand Vossler, Quentin Tarantino, and friends at a cookie-making house party. (Courtesy of Alan Sanborn)

did it in class. It was interesting. He didn't get very good reviews from the teacher! I tended to go big, so everyone else was on this kind of "big" level. But Quentin's whole thing was that it would be funnier to have the really crazy one be less intense and sort of more subdued. It was an interesting choice, but the teacher didn't think it worked very well.

Vossler soon enlisted his college filmmaking buddies to come work with he and Tarantino on *My Best Friend's Birthday*.

ALAN SANBORN: Rand invited me one night to Craig Hamann's house, where they were having a film meeting. Quentin and Craig were there. This was the first time I met Quentin and Craig. Craig seemed kind of self-possessed. I remember thinking he was very confident and very funny. I seem to remember him wearing a motorcycle jacket. Quentin was really into gay jokes at the time; jokes about the male anatomy and things of that nature. That really took me aback at first. I wasn't sure what to make of that. They were just telling me a little bit about the movie. Mostly they were all just joking around, as I recall. There was a lot more goofing around than there was talking about the movie.

Tarantino finding humor in dick jokes should come as no surprise when one considers this exchange in the famous "Like a Virgin" discussion in *Reservoir Dogs* (featuring Tarantino himself as Mr. Brown):

MR. BROWN: Dick, dick, dick, dick, dick, dick, dick, dick, dick.

MR. BLUE: How many dicks is that?

MR. WHITE: A lot.

ALAN SANBORN: I worked as a production assistant, mostly helping Rand, on one day of shooting. I remember Rand and Dov being there. We were shooting in someone's apartment somewhere. I remember very little about it except that I don't think I had all that great a time, and I don't remember being asked back. That production stuff—the assisting—was never really my strong suit.

CRAIG HAMANN: When we made *My Best Friend's Birthday*, Quentin and I didn't know what we were doing. Sometimes when people write about the movie on the Internet, they talk about how amateurish it is. They're right. We just jumped in there without any film school and started filming stuff, trying to put together a movie. And there's nothing wrong with that. Quentin has called it our film school, and I agree. That's exactly what *My Best Friend's Birthday* was. And we both felt it was better working on that than doing nothing, which is something I see a lot of people doing after they move to L.A. They talk about everything they're going to do, but they don't ever do it. So we just jumped in and did it.

QUENTIN TARANTINO: None of us knew what we were doing. We were all just fumbling around together and just trying to keep everybody there since we weren't paying them anything. Pioneer Chicken was our craft service.

TODD HENSCHELL: There were no contracts with anybody on that movie, which I think was fine because everyone was pretty much there for a single cause. I remember someone asking, "If we sell this, who gets paid what?" I said, "I don't need to be paid anything. I did this because we're friends. If everybody gets rich off this, you can give me some money if you want to. If you don't, I don't care." I really didn't either. It was a labor of love. None of us did that for money. That wasn't part of the deal.

ROGER AVARY: We had a very interesting combination of people working on that film. Craig was a charismatic guy with a background in acting. Rand Vossler was also very important on the project. He had a good eye behind the camera. Scott McGill was also a major participant on *My Best Friend's Birthday*. And a lot of people involved with those early films helped us on our movies later in life.

CRAIG HAMANN: I think everyone but me knew they would be directing a film one day. Quentin certainly did. Roger had already finished some great Super-8 films. Rand was very technically well-versed. I hadn't directed anything, and I was fairly technically illiterate. The tech side of things bores the shit out of me. Quentin was the same way. I don't think he was bored by the tech stuff, but he sure as hell was a lot more interested in the creative end. Of course, as you direct a film, you start to learn about the technical aspects.

RICHARD "RICK" SQUERI: We were happy to be shooting at a level much higher than we ever had before. This was a real film. This wasn't a video. This was the real thing. It was tooth-and-nails to get the crew, and people were wonderful and helped out, a few people from class helped out. I remember being on that set and thinking, "Wow, this is so great. We're finally doing this more professionally." At that time that seemed professional. I was happy to see that we were all maturing and getting closer to the real deal. I had been on film and TV sets at that point only in the stunt world. It was a very different relationship with things.

CRAIG HAMANN: You have to be very careful about casting friends, because if they're not professional actors, you're not going to get a professional performance. We certainly had incidents of that in the movie. You know, you have a lot of actors there doing a pretty good job, but then there's someone who maybe should have studied the role more, put the right preparation into it so it would have been a more professional performance. You also have to be very careful when you cast people's personalities. You don't need a prima donna on your set. We had one. But overall we were very, very fortunate to have a pretty good cast.

Casting is really important. Quentin has often said that casting is ninety-percent of directing. He's right. It is, without a doubt. When it comes to getting a performance out of an actor especially. If their performance isn't there for you to get, it isn't going to happen. That's why you need people who identify with the roles. John Travolta once told me he was interviewing for *The Last Detail*. He was being read and kept coming back repeatedly for the role Randy Quaid eventually played. He didn't get the role, obviously. He was told by the director that, "John, you're the most qualified person who read for the role, but when Randy Quaid walked into the room, he was the role." That's important when casting. You've got to put people together. Can they work together? And if someone comes in there and they are that role, then you have to cast

Crystal Shaw, Leeanne Chambers, Tarantino, and Craig Hamann during filming of the shower scene. (Courtesy of Todd Henschell)

them. We didn't really have the luxury to cast that way. We had to get who we could get.

CRYSTAL SHAW: I wanted to work with Quentin because he could see the scene, describe it, and he had vision about the projects and was so motivated. So I agreed to work in this second small film, *My Best Friend's Birthday*. My friends from acting school were like, "Are you going to do it?" I was like, "Yeah!" Everyone would tell me, "They need to pay you." That's what everyone used to say. And I said no. I had been stage acting since I was in junior high school. It doesn't pay. I had probably been the lead in about twenty musicals, and part of at least twenty more. That's how I grew up, doing stage work and musicals and summer stock. But I thought, the only people out here I was meeting had what I had—a college degree and some talent—but Quentin had drive, talent, and vision per project, per scene, per shot, and he had this way of making you feel confident. He just said, "You've really got this thing." Or he would say, "You know when you say that? That's unique. You have a unique way of speaking."

Quentin was like George Cukor, who was known for being a director of actresses. I told Quentin that, and I meant that as a genuine compliment. I always said Quentin should just work with women, because he had an amazing talent for that. He could explain things to you so well. For instance, there's a scene where Mickey is in the shower and Misty opens the shower door and sings happy birthday to Mickey and she says, "I'll wait in the other room and when you're done here, we'll party, oh, and keep it casual. What you have on is fine." I love that line.

I don't know if Quentin still does this, but he would take me aside and confidentially talk to me about the scene. I thought, what a great way of directing! When he did that, a couple of things happened. It was a very intimate moment and you feel very special. And keep in mind that in real life he was a video clerk and only twenty-something. So he'd shoot the scene just by watching you do your thing, and he'd usually get a kick out of how you did it your way. Often it was just what he loved. Then he might make a few suggestions privately, and after the scene was shot, he'd either smile at you, come hug you, or say that's it. But he'd already have the shot one way or the other. And we'd just matter-of-factly move on and we would set up for the next scene.

A lot of directors just say, "Can you speed up the lines?" "Can you slow down the dialogue?" "Let's all dig deeper." But Quentin would get specific. "Do me a favor. If you can this one time, just stare at him, but don't change your facial expression. And just shut the door." I love that scene and I love that line. I loved that direction and have used it in other situations. The dry delivery. He was such a great director.

When we were shooting *My Best Friend's Birthday* Quentin said, "You have a way of talking on the inhale instead of the exhale. Don't ever change that." I still don't know what that means, but who pays that much attention to someone's breathing? And he would tell me other actresses who also did that, and his advice left a lasting impression. He would give me references like the Nancy Allen character in *Blow Out* and other contemporary actors who were more natural at the time.

A publicity photo of actress Crystal Shaw from around the time *My Best Friend's Birthday* was made. (Courtesy of Crystal Shaw)

TODD HENSCHELL: Quentin was always kind of buoyant when he was filming, even if things weren't going well. That's a great trait to have. He had to deal with one of his actors... They were shooting at his mother's house in Torrance. It was either for sale or had been sold, and it was almost empty. They were going to do an all-night shoot because they were leaving the house the next day. Those were the scenes that I saw the most of. There were a couple of really funny scenes. There was one where an actress named Leanne opens the shower door to talk to Craig and she asks if he and Clarence are lovers. He says no and he slams the door. It's a hilarious scene. But there was a guy they had hired to play a cop. His name was David O'Hara, and David has some ideas about the power of actors on the set versus directors on the set.

QUENTIN TARANTINO: Literally, to this day, David O'Hara was the worst actor I've worked with. Well, not the worst *actor*, but he wasn't that good of an actor either. But he was definitely the most difficult.

TODD HENSCELL: He was just belligerent the whole time. He started telling Quentin what to do, and if you know Quentin, you know that's not a good practice. You know that old saying about "don't poke a bear with a stick"? Well, David was doing that all night long. I walked over to Craig and I said, "Quentin's gonna kick his ass." At some point he's just gonna snap. David was making offhand comments after every take. But the fact of the matter is that the things Quentin was telling him to do were the correct things. But David wouldn't do what Quentin wanted him to do and finally he said, "This is the last take." And Quentin said, "I'll tell you when it's the last take." It was a good thing David wasn't working for Stanley Kubrick or Francis Ford Coppola, who were infamous for using an excessive number of takes.

RAND VOSSLER: I remember it very distinctly: "This is the last take!" Quentin had an aggressive relationship with Dave. I think Dave was one of our more experienced actors—he had done some professional work. Because we were a skeleton crew, we would have long set ups and long hours and we were really pushing everybody.

And Dave just got fed up. I think we were shooting the sequence with him bursting through the door when that happened.

QUENTIN TARANTINO: To this day I still hear that in my brain. We were doing a take and I said, "I need you to do it one more time." And he goes, "This is the last take!" I still hear that in my head! Any time an actor gets kind of prickly on set I think to myself, "This is the last take!"

RAND VOSSLER: It became kind of a running joke on the set. Whenever we were getting close to the end of the day, someone would always say, "This is the last take!"

QUENTIN TARANTINO: We all quoted that for years, me, Craig, and Todd. We had a great time quoting David.

CRAIG HAMANN: Dave got mad and slowed everything down. Admittedly, it was very late, everyone was dead tired. However, the rest of us—people like Quentin, Rand, Scott, myself—we had been shooting all day before he arrived, and he was telling us how long the hours are for him. It just got to be unbearable. He and Quentin had words that night. Quentin was getting very impatient with Dave, and justifiably so. But Dave did stick around for the rest of the scene and everything got done.

DAVID O'HARA: Quentin had really strong opinions. He didn't argue much with me. To be honest, I never valued his opinion anyway. That's just me. Quentin had a personality that I was not attracted to. He talked too much. I was thirty-four, and he was seventeen or eighteen. I didn't give him much credit. He probably deserved more credit than I gave him. I just tossed it off like I was talking to a child. I did admire that he was very aggressive, opinionated, and had a lot of belief in himself. That's cool. Whenever you see him in an interview now, it's like, 'Wow! I've never seen him with that much belief in himself." I saw him in an interview talking about how "the American public is indebted to my parents. Without them, they wouldn't have had me. And without me, we wouldn't have had *Inglourious Basterds*." That is almost an exact quote. And I just go, you've got to be fucking kidding me! It wasn't Lawrence of fucking Arabia… I tried to watch *Inglourious Basterds* twice and I didn't like it. The scenes were too long.

CRAIG HAMANN: To be honest with you, I think casting Dave was a mistake on Quentin's part. Dave was really my friend more than anyone else's. I knew Dave. There were things about him I liked. He was a very aggressive person. Dave and I used to go into the studios and pass pictures of ourselves to leave on desks and we'd leave copies of our scripts. He was very aggressive in that way, and I admired that about him.

I told Quentin when I wrote the role of Eddie, I really wanted our friend Rick Squeri to do it, but Quentin said, "I think Dave could do this role well." I said, "No, don't cast him." It wasn't anything against Dave, but he and Quentin didn't really get along to begin with. I could only foresee friction there. And sure enough, it happened. It got to a point where we were thinking, "Oh, man, we need to recast this guy." We already had enough footage shot of him that it wouldn't be wise to do that. Unless we would have gotten financing to redo the whole movie… Then yeah, we would've recast. We would've paid an actor and gotten a much more professional attitude.

DAVID O'HARA: Quentin doesn't have much self-doubt. I thought he was pretty aggressive, which was fine. It was his movie. I don't remember how well he worked with the actors. I think they were pretty much on their own unless he gave them line readings or something. I don't really remember much about my scene. I wasn't a Method actor, but I used some Method stuff. I remember trying to do a scene and couldn't find out how to motivate the thing at all.

CRAIG HAMANN: The actress playing Cecilia was named Leeane. One of the problems we had with her was that she was Dave's girlfriend, and with Dave, every time he was there, he would get bored and expect us to move faster, despite the fact that we were having problems with the cameras and equipment. He

A shot of Leeane Chambers from the film. (Courtesy of Todd Henschell)

couldn't understand that. Then Leeane would get grumpy with us, which was getting on both Quentin's and my nerves. She was a nice person, and I don't mean to talk smack about her, but this was a no-budget movie, and I have to question the mental state of anyone who was there who couldn't understand that this was not going to be easy. And that was particularly true with Dave, who was just whining like a little bitch most of the time.

Tarantino would later refer to *My Best Friend's Birthday* as being his personal film school, and Hamann agrees with this assessment.

CRAIG HAMANN: The entire film was trial by fire. Long nights, no money, not much sleep, if any. But we learned a lot from just holding our noses and taking the plunge. In this way, *My Best Friend's Birthday* is a constant source of pride for me. I remember one asshole telling me that I'd never get the film done, and even if I did, it would be a piece of shit. I never told Quentin that the guy said this to me. But we did a good job, especially for two guys who didn't know what the hell we were doing. So I think it was a good thing. And it was, without a doubt, all the better because Quentin and I did it together, always relying on our faith in one another throughout the entire ordeal. I'm not trying to leave out Rand, Roger, or anyone else, but the truth is, Quentin and I were the ones who decided to take on the task of making the movie.

Another small hiccup in the production was a number of disagreements between filmmaker Byron Meyers, Tarantino, and Hamann. The duo, along with Crystal Shaw, had worked with him previously on *Sex Olympics*, which he'd directed/re-edited.

TODD HENSCHELL: During one scene there was a guy present who was there with Crystal Shaw. He was some guy named Byron. I don't know what their relationship was. And he was debating with Quentin, asking him why he wasn't shooting big master shots. Quentin said, "We're short on time and we don't need them." And really, master shots are kind of a crutch. You very rarely use any of them. Quentin kind of got that idea from Alfred Hitchcock who, when he first came to America, he was trying to stop the studios from recutting his films. He said, "If I don't give them the stuff to redo it, then they can't redo it." Byron said, "He did that because those guys were messing with him. Nobody's messing with you." Quentin said, "We don't need that footage anyway. So why waste the film? We're broke, so I'm gonna shoot what I need and that's it."

CRAIG HAMANN: Byron was a nice guy. He was a filmmaker. I liked him a lot. He had a great sense of humor and seemed to be able to read people well. But Todd is right. Byron did argue with Quentin on the set, and with me, too. Not about the film content, the script, or Quentin's direction, but because we kept running late, which was keeping Crystal up late. Byron was merely looking out for Crystal and never really made a big problem for Quentin and myself. And deep down inside, Byron understood the difficulties that come with guerrilla filmmaking. He had done it himself. So maybe they were more debates than arguments.

One aspect of low-budget guerrilla filmmaking that is almost always present is the need for adequate locations to film. Considerations have to be made regarding the price of the location—usually free, belonging to a friend of someone involved with the production—and also room enough for the crew and availability. Because of this, several scenes were filmed at the house of Tarantino's mother, Connie Zastoupil. ("Pretty much all of the scenes that take place at Clarence's apartment were shot at Connie's house," recalls Hamann.)

CONNIE ZASTOUPIL: At the time I thought of Quentin's interest in filmmaking as more of a hobby. I know that bothered him, but he was so young. I didn't know it would end up being a career, because the odds of making it in Hollywood are really stacked against you. When he told me he wanted to shoot at my house, I had visions of a handheld camera. So when they moved in with all the equipment, I said, "Oh dear!"

Zastoupil not only opened up her home for filming, but she also served as craft services on occasion. Crystal Shaw remembers Zastoupil as being "really young and adorable," and remembers her making everyone bologna sandwiches with Kool-Aid, potato chips, and chocolate chip cookies. Shaw says everyone working on the film was overjoyed to have food after many hours of filming. "That was a pretty big lunch for an actor back in those days," she says. "And it was free! That was actually amazing back in those days." Zastoupil says she's happy that Shaw remembers the food fondly, but now feels guilty for having fed the crew what she now considers unhealthy junk food.

CONNIE ZASTOUPIL: I ended up moving out for a couple of weeks. I was gone for quite some time. Rather than get upset or try to monitor what they were doing, I just did that. I stayed away until they were finished. And I think I stocked the refrigerator for them, but I can't really remember. I wasn't bothered by them using the house, and they were very, very respectful. And there was only the minimal amount of damage done, and it was probably far less than it should have been. They were very careful. One of the overhead bathroom fixtures got broken when they filmed in there. That was really all that got broken in my house. I thought they did a pretty good job, having that many people in there and it not being a movie set.

CRYSTAL SHAW: I remember Quentin's mom as only a twenty-something can, but I do remember thinking, "I wish my mom was more like that in a certain way." I'm from a family of six kids, and my mom was great. She was totally the *Leave It to Beaver* mom, but she would rarely do things on the spur of the moment. His mama raised Quentin in the most unique way. So I borrowed a page from her playbook in some ways.

Quentin used to talk about getting to go to the movies in the middle of a weekday. Wow. He loved movies so much that she followed his lead. My son was into computers and video games at a very young age. He was always trying to figure out the engineering of how things worked, and he loved video games. A lot of people would tell me, "He shouldn't be playing video games at four or five." Well, guess where my son is now traveling on his life's path? Computers. He actually built his first computer when he was fifteen, and he has a passion for them. By then, Quentin was working at what he loved, successfully, so the jury was in. And he was achieving success and happiness while doing it. So I thought, "You know what? Quentin's mom let him do the things he was interested in and look how he turned out."

CONNIE ZASTOUPIL: This is terrible, but in hindsight, I should have considered it more of a serious project instead of a hobby. If I had known these kids were this serious, I would have probably given them more money. I really didn't know. He was very enthusiastic, but he was enthusiastic about all aspects of the movies. I just really didn't know it was that serious. If I had known, I would have given him more money.

CRYSTAL SHAW: I hope Connie feels great about her parenting. Thank goodness she didn't interfere more or help him more on this movie, although I thought she was really supportive and let us hang out and stuff. Whatever ended up happening, the result was Quentin Tarantino. So thank God she didn't change a thing. Think about it: what if that one element had changed him in some way and made him say, "I can chill a little bit because I'll probably get help"? No. He had so much drive, and who knows what gave that to him? So whatever she did or didn't do, I think it was absolutely the right thing. He turned out amazing.

CRAIG HAMANN: There is a scene that takes place in a bar. When we were scouting for this movie, Quentin and I were going to bars like crazy. We were going in there trying to get someone to say, "Sure, yeah, you can shoot here." So we would go into these bars, have a couple of drinks, and then talk to the bartender and try to talk to the owner. One time we went to this one bar, sat at the table, went up to the bar counter, got some drinks, sat down at the table, and at the time that we sat down at the table, we looked around… It was a gay bar, and we hadn't known it. It was kind of a creepy gay bar that looked like it might be borderline leather, so we hustled out of there. We didn't even ask if we could shoot there.

Quentin ended up finding this guy who had a bar and he said, "You can shoot here, but you can only do it from about two in the morning until six. So it was real late for everybody that was there. Especially for those of us who were also shooting in the day. I mean, Quentin, Rand Vossler, Dov Schwarz, myself, Scott McGill… We had started shooting in the morning and had then gone right on through the whole day, right on through the whole night. Then we'd go home and try to get as much sleep as we could, which was never very much. Then we were all back shooting all through the day again and would end up at that bar again in the wee hours of the morning. It was very difficult that way, but it was a lot of fun.

RAND VOSSLER: We had carte blanche to film whatever we needed in the bar. Somebody knew the owner. It started out where we could show up after hours or right before the bar closed and bring our equipment in and set it up. Once the place cleared out, we would have free rein. After the first couple of times we shot there, it got to the point where the owner would just give us the keys and say, "Lock up when you guys are done. I'm not waiting around." Finally, it got to where we would let ourselves in and shoot during their off hours and then be gone by six a.m. when people would come in and clean up. It was some of our most loose, free production time because we had a great location and we had complete freedom; so much so that we would go into the walk-in cooler and make ourselves sandwiches. And there was a dark room there where I could change the film reels.

CRAIG HAMANN: One of the things I liked about that bar was the ambiance. It works really well in black and white. It was a good place for us to shoot at, it really was. I think it was in Torrance. If it wasn't, it was right next to it. Almost everything we shot was in Torrance, California.

RAND VOSSLER: After our initial shooting period, we went to shooting on weekends and shooting late nights at the bar and shooting for seventy-two-hour periods, and eventually our crew dwindled down to myself, Dov Schwarz, and Craig. People just stopped showing up and we were working with a skeleton crew.

While working on the film, Tarantino had an inspired idea. He cast Allen Garfield, his acting teacher at the time, as baker Bill Smith (named after one of Tarantino's favorite actors, William Smith). Garfield was an accomplished actor of both television and film, with credits as diverse as Woody Allen's *Bananas* and *Beverly Hills Cop II*.

Taking this casting idea a step further, Tarantino called up his former acting coach Brenda Hillhouse, who had since retired from acting and had found a new career in advertising, to appear as Garfield's wife. Tarantino had always been fond of Hillhouse, frequently complimenting her and telling her she was his favorite actress. The

A shot of Allen Garfield between takes. (Courtesy of Todd Henschell)

fact that he later cast her in *Pulp Fiction, From Dusk Till Dawn*, and his 1995 "Mother's Day" episode of *E.R.* bears this out. "That's very meaningful that he said those things and that he sought me out for those projects," she says. "Especially since my acting dreams had faded away and my life had become something different."

Rand Vossler, Tarantino, Brenda Hillhouse, and Allen Garfield prepare for a scene inside Video Archives, which doubles here as a bakery. (Courtesy of Todd Henschell)

BRENDA HILLHOUSE: Quentin called me out of the blue and said he was making *My Best Friend's Birthday*. They were going to be shooting all night, and there was a scene he wanted me to do with Allen Garfield. I said, "Sure, I'll do it." So I went down there, and we shot all night long after the video store had closed. I'm hardly in the edited footage that exists. I'm barely there, but it was a fun night. I think that's the reason Quentin called me in later for *Pulp Fiction*, because I had done him this favor and he remembered it.

The scene with Garfield and Hillhouse was an interesting one as it was shot inside Video Archives, which was given a face-lift to appear as a bakery. "I still love that you can see a *Runaway Train* standee in the scene," recalls Tarantino. The filming of the scene is notable for two reasons: Roberto A. Quezada worked as the film's cinematographer for the scene, and also because veteran actor Garfield appears in it.

RAND VOSSLER: Scott McGill had started working on the Don Coscarelli film *Survival Quest*, and Roberto Quesada was the DP on that. Scott brought me on *Survival Quest*, and there was a long production gap on *My Best Friend's Birthday*. We went back into production on the stuff Quentin had written to extend the film to feature-length. "Since we've got access to a professional DP for this scene with Allen Garfield, should we get Roberto to come and work on the project?" So I said, "Sure, let's do that. Why not?" And Roberto was more than happy to come do that.

Our experience with that was not positive. He only worked on that one scene. We had Allen there in some of the worst-looking footage in the piece. I think it was mostly due to the lighting. We were so limited in our resources, and the style and look of the film was very basic, with strong rim lights and kind of source-y key lights. And Roberto came in and we had a Lowel kit, no flags or scrims, and the space was kind of bigger. By the time that shoot could come around, we were such a well-oiled machine that we could get to our locations to shoot and were up and running quickly. Everybody knew our roles, and we actually had a better camera for that shoot because we were able to access stuff from the camera department at L.A. City College. So when Roberto joined that environment, he was the one trying to play catch-up. We were needing things to happen quickly, and if you look at the footage from that night, it's not our strongest. Quentin told me later that he felt it was a mistake to bring Roberto in.

CRYSTAL SHAW: I kind of remember some mention of an actor named Allen Garfield who would be working on *My Best Friend's Birthday*. Before he arrived, there were mixed impressions of him. I remember thinking, "I have no idea who this person is." I really didn't know. But I wasn't a big movie buff back then. I remember thinking, "I wish I knew who this guy was, because everybody's talking about him." There was no Google back then. I remember glancing at him before he did his scene. I had a job and I had to leave, so I couldn't stay, but I remember thinking, "I'll have to watch this guy's movies and see who he is."

BRENDA HILLHOUSE: Allen kind of gave Quentin a hard time on the shoot. I think it was because he'd been Quentin's teacher, and because there was a lot of improvising that night. I don't think he liked that. I'm the kind of person that I'll do anything

Fill-in cameraman Roberto Quesada shooting the bakery scene. (Courtesy of Todd Henschell)

for anybody, but Allen was different. He had his own way of doing things, and those weren't necessarily the way Quentin wanted them done. So Allen kind of tried to take over the scene.

ROGER AVARY: I remember seeing Allen Garfield on the set and saying, "Holy crap! That's Allen Garfield from *The Stunt Man*!" Allen had some issues with the way we were doing things, but it wasn't anything personal. He came from a different world. We were just neophytes making a movie, whereas he was a guy who had worked extensively in Hollywood. He was an acting teacher at the time, and he sort of turned into an acting teacher on that film instead of being an actor. It was just his natural instinct.

CRAIG HAMANN: Despite the fact that he had the experience, and despite the fact that he was a wonderful actor, what Allen Garfield wasn't getting in step with was the fact this was a no-budget movie. We simply did not have the time for him to be asking someone a question about the character and about why he was doing this stuff. I don't know why he was doing that. It was almost like he was deliberately giving Quentin a bit of a problem. Maybe he felt like he was teaching Quentin as he was giving him this problem, you know? And if he did feel that way, I don't know why, because from a directing standpoint, Quentin knew more than he did, even at that time. Allen felt that nobody could direct the way he could, and I don't agree with that, although he was a great actor. So yeah, that was a tough shoot that night. It was a long night. It was one that could've been cut a little shorter if Allen hadn't gone on and on and on with question after question.

Also, Allen got there late. It wasn't his fault, though. I'm trying to remember what happened. I think it was Stevo Polyi or somebody—someone picked him up and their car didn't work. I had to run out to get all of them. And Allen brought his little dog with him, which was fine. The dog didn't get in the way at all, and it was a really sweet little dog.

QUENTIN TARANTINO: Allen Garfield wasn't challenging on the set at all. Everybody thinks that because they had never done anything before. They had no idea what working with a terrific actor who was donating his time and working all night for free was supposed to be like. Not only was he working all night for free on this amateur production, but he was actually breaking the SAG rules to do it. He wasn't demanding it, it was just that that night was Allen Garfield night, so everything revolved around him.

I was so excited to have him there because he was one of my favorite character actors of the time. The truth is, he was the best acting teacher I've ever had, by far, frankly. Jack did a good job, too, but Allen was in a class of his own. What he did was just amazing. I was very familiar with his work for Coppola and his work with De Palma, and we got along great in acting class. He was really terrific in acting class. I told him I wanted to act, but I wanted to be a director. And he said, "Okay, then I will treat you both as an actor and as a director." Then when we started the class, he said, "Everybody, this is Quentin Tarantino. He's in this class, but he wants to be a director. And I have no doubt he's going to be a fantastic director. So if you do a scene with Quentin, Quentin is the director. It is your job to take direction from Quentin. It's Quentin's job to come up with the tone of the scene. You are to listen to what he says. If you do a scene with Quentin, Quentin is the director. That's what time it is. And I'm holding Quentin responsible for the scene you guys do together." That was fucking awesome!

But also, to this day, Allen was one of the great improvisational actors of his time. Allen would do improvs that were magnificent. He's one of the greatest improv actors of all time. And if you want to see it, just watch his movies for De Palma, which were all improvisation. The entire five-minute scene in *Greetings* with him and Robert DeNiro, all improvisation. So I had a little script for Allen, and then he would just extrapolate from it. That's what I wanted because that's what they did in Brian De Palma's *Greetings*. One of my favorite things in *Greetings* are those jump cut scenes. He's playing the big scene and then you just kind of jump cut to the best parts of it. I kind of liked that '60s style anyway, so I thought, "This will be my chance to do that. And I'll do it with Allen Garfield from *Greetings*. That'll be fucking awesome!" To me it was the equivalent of me being De Niro playing opposite Allen Garfield in *Hi Mom* or in *Greetings*, so I chopped it up that way. And I was very, very happy with it.

Allen Garfield was fantastic. He did me a tremendous solid. He was awesome, and it's the best scene in the movie. I'll always appreciate what he did. It was the first time I ever worked with someone who was not just a professional actor, but a really great actor.

RUSSELL VOSSLER: I remember coming into the store that day and watching them work on the movie. Part of it was shot there, and the glass counter was decorated to look like a bakery for a scene in the movie.

TODD HENSCHELL: Allen Garfield was in the scene and he brought his dog with him. I said, "Hey Quentin, you gotta get the dog in there! Put him up on the counter." I thought the dog should be in the room during the scene because the dog was cute. So they did some shots of the dog.

QUENTIN TARANTINO: Allen was one of those guys who had a little dog that he carried everywhere with him. He's one of those dudes, all right?

TODD HENSCHELL: There was this birthday cake on the counter. It was the cake Quentin was going to buy for his best friend. They were doing the scene and they finished one take. I looked down and I said, "You don't have to eat that cake later, do you?" Quentin said, "Why?" I said, "The dog just ate half of it." The dog had climbed into the glass cabinet and was eating the cake. Half of it was gone, so it was going to be a continuity problem.

QUENTIN TARANTINO: We looked down and the dog was on this lower counter eating the goddamn cake!

When asked what his favorite experience on the film was, Tarantino doesn't hesitate to say it was working with Garfield. But then he takes it a step further, explaining why.

QUENTIN TARANTINO: There were only two times when we were working on *My Best Friend's Birthday* that it really felt like we were making a movie, as opposed to just getting together and screwing around, since we didn't know what we were doing. One

Allen Garfield's dog on set inside Video Archives. (Courtesy of Todd Henschell)

of those was working with Allen Garfield that night in the video store. That was my favorite memory from the shoot also. The other was the very last scenes we shot, which was the radio station stuff. When I say *My Best Friend's Birthday* was like my film school, it really was. I worked on that for three years, and the majority of the stuff that deals with the story itself is the stuff we shot the first week, while I was still learning how to direct a movie. That's just what that is. But after shooting for two to three years, and I had written a bigger sequence involving the radio station...bigger than what we had done previously... So I had kind of learned how to do it. By that point and time, by the time it came to that silly radio station scene, I knew how to shoot it. I knew what I was doing. And it looked fairly professional. I mean, it's just a two-shot and this and that, but it flowed. That was the first time I felt I had learned something from the process. So those were the two big moments for me. The Allen Garfield thing was incredibly exciting, both acting in a scene with him and also working with a terrific actor. Having him at Video Archives was groovy.

CRAIG HAMANN: You know what's weird about that scene? On the Internet Movie Database, they have Allen Garfield listed

Clarence (Tarantino) and Bill Smith (Allen Garfield) discuss what can and cannot be put on Mickey's cake. (Courtesy of Todd Henschell)

as "Entertainment Magnate." That's what his character is listed as. That wasn't what he was at all. He was Bill Smith, who owned a video bakery store. I don't know why they thought he was Entertainment Magnate. I don't understand that at all. The dialogue being the way it was, this big, intense argument over Elvis Presley, and the fact Clarence wants Bill to write this entire poem on the cake, which is not possible... I don't know how anyone gets Entertainment Magnate from that.

RAND VOSSLER: One of my pet peeves is the misinformation out there on the Internet about *My Best Friend's Birthday*. There were two cinematographers on the film: Scott and myself. But it looks like there were four. Roberto shot for one night, and according to Wikipedia, Roger Avary was a cameraman, too. But he never was. That's wrong.

CRYSTAL SHAW: One day Quentin and I were doing a cute little getting to know you, first kiss scene for our characters, Misty and Clarence. We were in a tent we made out of blankets in his room. Similar to the type of tents children make to play indoors when it's raining outside. In the scene, Quentin and I leaned into a kiss, and I leaned into a light bulb and burnt my cheek. And Quentin and Craig were like, "Crystal, stop, stop, you need to stop, sweetie!" I had not seen the burn yet and it didn't feel like much. But they made me stop and look at the burn. They took me off set to go sit over to the side. They brought me ice packs and wanted to see how bad it was. Then Quentin came over and was holding my hands and telling me, "We can start again tomorrow. Let's take a break for the day. We can start again tomorrow. Let's keep ice on that." And Craig brought me more ice.

I just said to both of them, "I think I'm okay. Let's try makeup." So I just reapplied some makeup. I saw Quentin and Craig go to the corner and talk about it, and then they came back and said, "It's totally up to you, Crystal. We can wait until tomorrow. It's no big deal." At this point in my career I had mostly been doing theatre, and the motto for theatre is "the show must go on..." So I said, "No, no, come on. Let's just go for it." After I did the scene, everybody was applauding and Quentin said he was really proud of me. And Craig said it was a great scene.

It was a burn, but just a little lightbulb burn, and we were all so freaking young. What did we know? I mean, if you're on the playground and you fall down and skin your knees, you just get up and keep playing.

Clarence (Tarantino) and Misty (Crystal Shaw) share a kiss. (Courtesy of Todd Henschell)

CRAIG HAMANN: People say that the acting is amateurish, and it is to some extent. There are actors that aren't really actors trying to help us out. There were times when we had people scheduled to come and do these roles and you'd be waiting an hour, two hours, they didn't show up, and finally you realize they aren't coming. You have to call friends up, and Quentin would have to rehearse them quickly and get them to memorize as much as they could. Feed them lines as the scene was going on. So yeah, there is a lot of amateurish acting in there, mainly because things were going south on us as far as getting actors.

There was one night where I remember having to wait several hours to begin. This was very late in the night. I forget where we were, but we were going to shoot a scene, but we had to find actors. People were supposed to be there, but again, they didn't show up. And it took us almost three hours to get people there. And even once they got there, we're pulling people out of bed, you know? So once they got there, Quentin's got to rehearse them and have them look at their lines. Quentin's trying to tell them what's happening in the scene... Then, action! We're shooting.

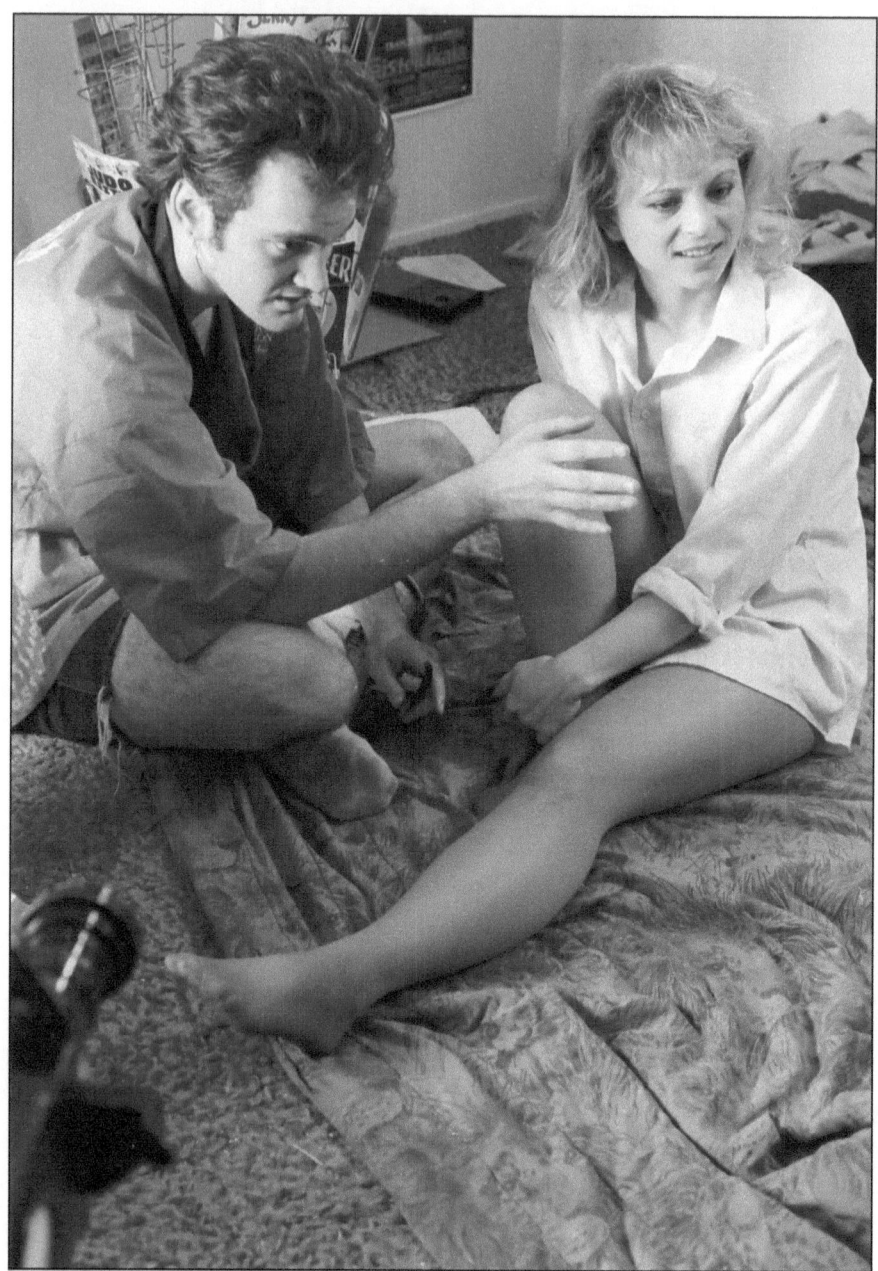

Tarantino and Crystal Shaw between takes of their romance scene. (Courtesy of Todd Henschell)

LINDA KAYE: Quentin asked me one night to be in the movie. All I had to do was sit on this guy's lap. This was in the mid-'80s, around '86 or '87. He asked me to be in it. The scene took half the night. It was in somebody's apartment over in a very scary part of town. Sort of Imperial Highway near Aviation, or Inglewood. That was the neighborhood. I think it might have been one of Quentin's old apartments when he lived in sort of a badass black neighborhood, for lack of a better term. This scene was supposed to take an hour, and it took about seven. And I remember I was late going over to my boyfriend's that night, and he got so mad at me that we had this huge fight that ended up leading to our breaking up. And I came back to Quentin's all upset. Quentin was involved in the film and all of its little problems. We had lighting problems and the neighbors kept banging on the ceiling saying, "*Shut the fuck up!*" I mean, this was at two in the morning and we were still at it, saying the same lines over and over. That had to get old for neighbors after a while.

ALAN SANBORN: One night I'm at home, and I got this call around 11 p.m. It was Rand and he says, "We're shooting right up the street from you." It was literally just up my block. "We were shooting a scene, and we had an actress who didn't show up. We need you to come play her part." I said, "You know I'm male, right?" He said, "Yeah, but it's a receptionist part, so we can just make it a man." I said, "Sure." I went over there and I took several different shirts with me so Quentin could pick which one he liked. They told me that in other scenes they'd already shot, the receptionist had been referred to or spoken to on the phone as Meg. So Quentin says, "You'll be Nutmeg!" So that's where the name Nutmeg came from.

Quentin looked at my shirts and he picked this wacky pumpkin shirt I had. It was a black shirt with pumpkins on it, and that's what I wore in the movie. There was a script, but I remember that scene being mostly improvisational; definitely the part in my scene where I had to start swearing like a banshee was improvised. Quentin just told me to just start cursing, so I did.

It should be noted that years later, when Tarantino invited Sanborn to appear as an extra in the coffee shop scene in *Reservoir Dogs*, he once again wore the "wacky pumpkin shirt" from *My Best Friend's*

Birthday. As Sanborn sees it, Nutmeg is actually the person eating there in the diner. As silly or as flippant as that idea might sound on its surface, it makes for pretty cool trivia. It also connects the $5,000 amateur film to the shared universe that Tarantino says exists in many of his other films. "Alan and I talked about that once," says Tarantino. "It's definitely Meg in *Reservoir Dogs*. And not only that, but Alan is sitting right next to my girlfriend from the time."

ALAN SANBORN: I remember Quentin telling me one time, "Every time you come on stage, I just get excited! There's something about you!" So I thought, oh, wow, that's cool! So I was excited to act for Quentin. But when I was performing in that scene, he kept asking me to tone it down and scale it back. I was surprised. He just wanted me to be very basic. He didn't want me to put very much emotion into it. That's why my character is so subdued, almost one note. But that's how he wanted me to do it. I felt like I was almost speaking monotone.

We shot that scene for most of the night. I think they were shooting another scene in the next room also.

Quentin was very energetic. He was very much into what he was doing. In both his direction and in talking to Quentin, he has this kind of crazy energy. He's always just very excited about whatever he's talking about. That's definitely infectious. I think he gets people excited about what they're doing just because he's so excited.

Because of the intermittent filming of *My Best Friend's Birthday*, the cast and crew were often on long hiatuses from the project. At one point, Crystal Shaw ended up moving out of state. When it was time to resume filming, Tarantino had to call her and beg for her to return. The only problem was that he couldn't pay her—not even for airfare—and by this time she had appeared in the hit Hollywood film *Hardbodies*.

CRYSTAL SHAW: I acted professionally in Hollywood off and on in the eighties. Then I went to visit my sister in Texas and ended up getting a third-grade teaching job there. The plan originally was just that I would work as a substitute teacher for a week, but they ended up hiring me for the year. So I thought, why not? What do I have to lose? Since all I was being offered by way of film was more bikini and horror movies, I took the teaching job and was able to do more theatre while I was there.

A few months later, I got a call from Quentin saying, "We're shooting some scenes. Can you come back to shoot some more? Please, please, please?" And I thought, man, I have such a good feeling about this project... But never in a million years did I think what happened to Quentin would happen. When shooting, there were camera shots I had never seen done before. I think Roger shot the scene where Clarence and Misty are playing pool. That was so cool. The shot went around us and that pool table while we just tried to act normally and lean in here and there, just doing the regular scene. That was an amazing shot! I pulled it up on YouTube the other day because I wanted to see some of the film and I still think it is one of my favorite camera shots. I love it.

It was such an easy film to be on, and it was just a weekend of shooting, and the reason I paid for the airline ticket to go back to L.A. was because it was fun and I was learning so much. I couldn't wait to get back on set. There are very few films I've worked on where I walked away saying, "Oh my God, that was so much fun!"

I had just finished *Hardbodies*, and it was huge at the time. Now it's kind of a classic, thank God. But at the time I was so embarrassed by that film because I had done a lot of classical stage work prior to that. But I wanted to get in the movies so I said I'd do the film even though they were like, "Your character has to wear a bikini." So when I got back to work on *My Best Friend's Birthday* the second time, I got a whole other level of respect. It was cool on the set and reuniting with people. The film was pretty much all guys, and I was in *Hardbodies*... Do I need to say more? They were like, "We saw you in the movie. You were so good! Wow!" Their reactions were really sweet and endearing.

Coinciding with the shoot, Tarantino and Hamann conceived a number of other ideas for movies they wanted to make. One concept they collaborated on, ultimately writing a treatment for, was a project called *The Criminal Mind*. This was a crime story about cops investigating a series of murders committed by a serial killer who has inexplicably stopped killing. "*The Criminal Mind* was mostly all Quentin's idea, much more so than mine," admits Hamann. "I helped fill in things, and I physically wrote it up, but that was an idea Quentin had come to me with. He came up with the blueprint and I helped build the rest of the house."

Not surprising, one pre-fame Tarantino solo effort was modeled as an Asian action picture of the John Woo variety. His treatment, titled *The Neon Jungle*, told the story of a hotel heist gone awry, resulting in tense *The Killer*-inspired Mexican standoffs. Hamann says Tarantino's interest in the project was short-lived. "I don't think that was ever really on his front burner," says Hamann. "I think when he finished writing it, he had other things he wanted to do. But for a while there, it was really important to Quentin that he do some sort of Asian action film—something with that influence." Another Tarantino script idea was called *Undercover Elvis*. "That was during Quentin's rockabilly days. He wanted to play Elvis Presley, who had faked his death because he was working undercover. I think if he had done that, it probably would have been a big hit. I remember the first time he pitched it to me, I laughed the whole time. I just thought that was great."

Hamann believes Tarantino became sidetracked, and eventually lost interest in these projects. "There were a lot of things happening for him in the late 1980s, one thing after another, like dominoes falling, that diverted his attention."

RAND VOSSLER: There were different periods of time when *My Best Friend's Birthday* was edited. We initially shot and shot and shot, and we didn't have money to process the footage. So there was a long period of time before we were able to get the money together to process everything from that initial period. That was something like 7,000 feet of film. Then we realized that the camera hadn't been working correctly and everything we had filmed up to that point was completely out of sync.

Craig had a buddy at Armand Hammer Films who let us work there. They had a flatbed, and the only way to put the film back in sync was to sit there and painstakingly go through every single frame.

Tarantino, Rand Vossler, and Craig Hamann hang out with Elvis. (Courtesy of Todd Henschell)

QUENTIN TARANTINO: I made a deal to work with this assistant editor [at Armand Hammer] who was interested in being my editor. We were told we could do this after hours. But we never got around to doing any of that.

RAND VOSSLER: We were given sort of an editor, but we had to do the work ourselves since we were doing it for free. This was training for her. That lasted for maybe four or five days before she lost interest in it.

QUENTIN TARANTINO: Basically, we ended up just fixing the sync on the movie. We had to cut it into sync. That took so long that by the time we were finished she was like, "Get the fuck out of here!"

RAND VOSSLER: That's when Quentin started doing the cutting.

QUENTIN TARANTINO: The editing that happened with the movie was all done by me. None of that was done by anyone else. I talked my mom into renting me a Steinbeck for a few weeks. I moved it into my apartment and I started editing the footage together.

RAND VOSSLER: At that point Quentin was disappointed in not getting enough footage and not shooting enough angles. Subsequently Quentin would say *My Best Friend's Birthday* was his film school, and it really was that kind of experience for him. He had a realization while cutting the film of just how that part of filmmaking worked.

QUENTIN TARANTINO: I was under the impression that we were making this really amazing thing. I was gonna be Jim Jarmusch and Spike Lee combined when *My Best Friend's Birthday* came out! Because *Stranger Than Paradise* and *She's Gotta Have It* were the examples of what could be done. I was sure this was gonna be the shit. That's why I worked for three years on it. And I never saw any footage the entire time we were shooting, because it was always in the lab. We didn't see any of it, we just kept shooting for those three years. So finally, I got the footage and started cutting it together, and upon reviewing all the footage from beginning to end, I realized I did not have what I thought I had. It wasn't really worth all of that. It wasn't that great. It was what it was. Because it was originally gonna be a short film, we had one week of shooting at the beginning, and that was more or less the crux of the story of the movie. Then I'd gotten the idea to turn it into a feature, and then it was just a matter of coming up with new scenes to keep adding to that structure.

So the thing is, that story stuff that's the spine of the story, was the footage that was the most embarrassing. It's because that literally was my first week of learning how to make a movie. And it's not like anyone else on the set knew how to make a movie.

I realized I didn't quite have what I thought I had... It might have been different if I didn't have about three Mt. Everests in front of me. Because I had no money. There were costs like getting a negative cutter. All the lab stuff in front of me was just so daunting that it probably would have taken me another two years to just finish post-production on it. And I wouldn't have been able to just do that a little bit at a time. It was just a thing where I realized this was not worth putting two or three more years of my life into.

I was very depressed for a little bit. I really had a big failure, because for three years everyone knew I was making this movie. This is what I was going to do. And now all of a sudden, I realized it was not very good and I was not gonna finish it. So it was a horrible, embarrassing failure. And I thought, "Well, you can like movies, but I guess that doesn't mean you know how to do them. I guess maybe I don't have it." But I'm a pretty optimistic guy. So after I gave myself a couple weeks of feeling really bad about myself, then I started getting out of it. I started looking at it more practically. I said, "Look, the footage that you're particularly embarrassed by is the footage from the first week." Well, that was when you didn't know what the fuck you were doing. But if you look at the last stuff you did, that's pretty fucking good." It cut together good and everybody's funny in it. It's a funny little scene. It's like wow, if you look at the stuff I did that first week and then you look at the stuff I did three years later, you can actually see a gigantic difference in the quality.

I thought, if this just ends up being a film school, it was a pretty fun film school, and it was a pretty cheap film school. So I ended up learning a lot. So I did get better, so that's good.

Shortly thereafter, Tarantino allegedly told crew members that a substantial portion of the existing film had been destroyed in a lab fire, forcing him to shut down production. However, there was no fire. According to Rand Vossler, Tarantino decided he didn't want to work on the film anymore and concocted the story.

RAND VOSSLER: The fire never happened. We did lose some footage, but the fire never happened. When we processed the initial batch of footage at Hollywood Film Enterprises, which was a lab in Hollywood that dealt with black-and-white footage, there was a power outage. Approximately one-and-a-half reels of our original footage was destroyed. It was in the developer too long and it turned white. So there was no lab fire. That was completely fabricated, but that was back when Quentin kind of embellished his story a little bit. I still have that footage. The tough part was that we lost a crucial scene with Al Harrell that took place in the bar and at that point we had already lost that location. We talked about ways we might reshoot that stuff somewhere else rather than being in the bar, but that was something that just never wound up happening.

QUENTIN TARANTINO: A lab fire didn't destroy the movie. A couple of rolls were destroyed. I don't remember specifically how many, whether it was two or four or six. These were minute-and-a-half rolls. And frankly, if they hadn't destroyed those rolls, I probably wouldn't have ever had the money to get the film out of the lab. They had destroyed so many rolls that they gave us a discount.

For the record, I never actually said the movie was destroyed in a fire. That just became part of the mythology. I started reading it in the biographies, and I figured, why not just go along with it? It was an interesting story, so I never corrected it.

RAND VOSSLER: Very clearly Quentin did not want this to be released. Eventually he did Reservoir Dogs, and that was one of the greatest directorial debuts ever. So then why would you wanna introduce this as your first film when you've already hit a home run? And that makes sense to me.

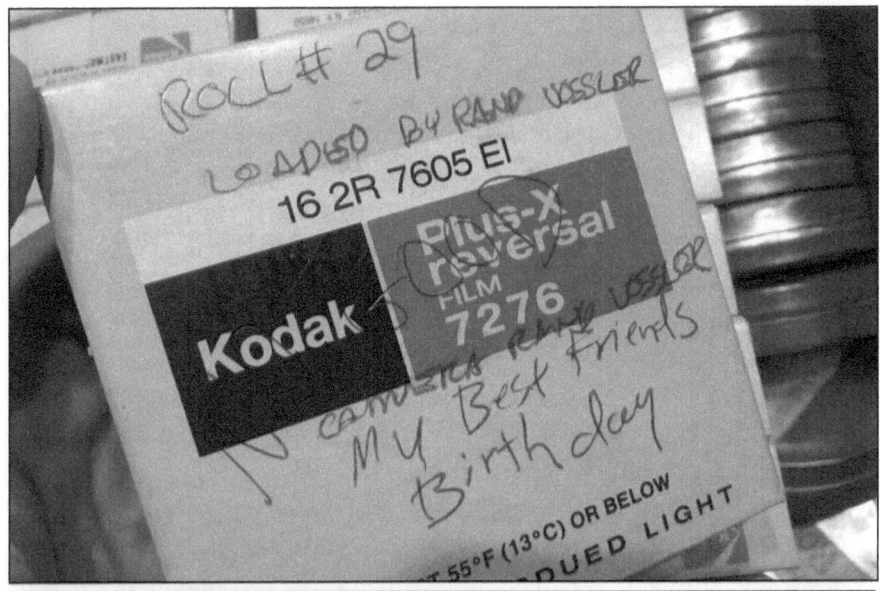

This is *My Best Friend's Birthday* as it exists today, in its unedited form. (Courtesy of Rand Vossler)

QUENTIN TARANTINO: When I realized I didn't have a movie, I edited my favorite scenes. That's the twenty-minute reel you see today. I didn't want to put the whole movie together. I still have the footage. It's sitting in storage. I could finish the movie one of these days. I might still do it, just to have it.

I have to say, I hadn't watched the movie in a long, long time, and then I ended up watching it about four years ago. It started, and it wasn't the way I remembered it starting off, but I was watching it, and it was just going on, and going on, and then, at some point in the movie, maybe three-quarters of the way into it, I started getting caught up in it. I started kind of caring about what was going on. I started watching it like a movie, and then, all of a sudden, it's over! It just stops! And I was like, "Whoa! Whoa! Whoa! What happened?" And one of the things that works so good about that twenty minutes is that I think it does eventually grab you. And then just when it grabs you, it's over. But it's not over, not finished, it's just like you're not allowed to see the rest. "Hey, wait a minute! I was watching that! What's going on?" So I was like, "Wow, this is pretty good." I actually got caught up in it. One of my favorite reviews that was ever written for my movies was by that dude who runs *Shock Cinema* [Steve Puchalski]. It was really funny. He was like, "This is subpar student filmmaking, but you know what? It's all there—all of the touchstones are already there! And goddammit, by the time the movie cuts out, I actually gave a fuck about what was going on!" [Laughs.] He said, "I actually wanted to see what was going to happen to Clarence and Mickey! I wanted to know who Misty Knight was gonna end up with."

My Best Friend's Birthday was originally intended to be a calling card for a would-be filmmaker with no credits. But once Tarantino started selling scripts and had established legitimate Hollywood credits, the calling card concept no longer made sense. Tarantino and the others who worked on this film have frequently called it their own private film school, and that summation seems apt. At the time he made this film, Tarantino was still a young artist in search of a voice and style. While elements of the voice and style he would later grow into are certainly present in this script, it appears to be something different from the type of films he ultimately wanted to be known for. While his humorous banter and frequent pop culture references are present, there's only a single gun to be found in *My Best Friend's Birthday*, and no one gets shot. That may sound flippant and demeaning toward Tarantino's work, but it's not intended to be—I made this observation to him when we spoke.

Tarantino himself has joked that he's become known as "the gun guy," and that's true. He's become a cinematic Jim Thompson, painting his art with a brush dipped in blood. At this point in his career it's difficult to imagine him making another screwball comedy. As *My Best Friend's Birthday* proves, he is capable of doing it and doing it well, but that doesn't seem to be the path he wants to take.

ROGER AVARY: Even though *My Best Friend's Birthday* was never completed, I don't look at it as a failure in any way. Things just sort of fell apart over time. Bigger things were starting to happen and the expense of it was overwhelming.

TODD HENSCHELL: We had a bunch of talented people who all pulled together trying to do something worthwhile. That's never a bad collection of memories to have. Except for the final sad one, which is that nobody will ever get to see the final product. A real tragedy, that.

QUENTIN TARANTINO: I might show *My Best Friend's Birthday* to a friend, but I would never show it to someone who might hire me for a job directing. It might be the reason they don't hire me! [Laughs.] I once had a producer who, after I'd showed him the tape, say, "Quentin, what you need to do with this tape is, you need to wrap it in the bloodiest steak you can find, and you need to get a little boat, and you need to go out into the ocean and find the sharkiest waters you can find, and then drop this meat-covered tape into the ocean!"

So I hadn't really thought much about it for a long time, and then years later, after I'd done *Reservoir Dogs* and *Pulp Fiction*, I was at the Munich Film Festival. And there was a young filmmaker there with his first film. It was Kevin Smith and the movie was *Clerks*. So I met Kevin and I met his producing partner, and they were really groovy, really cool. They said, "You were a big influence on us. We worked in video stores, too. *Reservoir Dogs* was cool, and we can't wait to see your movie." So I went and watched *Clerks*, and for the first time in my life I thought, maybe I should have finished *My Best Friend's Birthday*. And then afterward we went out drinking and I told them that story. They laughed and

Kevin said, "You made *Pulp Fiction* and then you're sitting watching *Clerks* and you think, 'I got something like that in my garage!'" [Laughs.] "What the fuck am I doing?"

Because of the continuity errors and amateurish nature of *My Best Friend's Birthday*, it's akin to *The Other Side of the Wind*, a film left unfinished at the time of director Orson Welles' death. As was the case with that, *My Best Friend's Birthday* could not possibly live up to the unrealistic expectations that have been placed on it, and therefore it's more important as a legendary unseen project than it would be if it was somehow completed and released today. But the screenplay is another matter altogether. Tarantino and Hamann's script is nothing short of magnificent. The dialogue crackles on the page. On paper, the project isn't hampered by the occasional acting misstep by an amateur performer or by makeshift locations such as a video store doubling as a bakery. The screenplay is brilliant and deserving of recognition for both writers.

Years later, Hamann optioned the script to producer Don Murphy, who had at that time established himself as Tarantino's most outspoken adversary. Murphy had been extremely vocal about Tarantino in a variety of public forums, eventually leading to Tarantino famously "bitch slapping" him in the posh West Hollywood eatery Ago, leading to a substantial lawsuit that was later settled. Contrary to stories stating otherwise, Hamann did not profit from the option, which basically gave Murphy control of the script for free in exchange for a chance to work on the project. "I didn't make any money off the deal at all," Hamann explains. "I got nothing out of it other than the chance to talk to Quentin again. That was kind of cool. We kind of touched base after that and saw each other a couple times. That was kind of nice."

DON MURPHY (*Natural Born Killers* producer): The comedies that I like best, be it *Heathers* or whatever, are just over the top... with a real sense of humor. And it was written by them [Tarantino and Hamann] to make as a modern-day screwball comedy, which still hasn't been done in a long time. I mean, *The Waterboy* and all this other crap out there is really not a modern-day screwball comedy, which is what this is. It's like circumstance leads to circumstance leads to circumstance.

Murphy once told the author of this book (way back in 1999) that his reasons for optioning the script were less than pure, saying he simply sought to annoy Tarantino. Nevertheless, Murphy's assessment of the screenplay's quality is accurate.

QUENTIN TARANTINO: The script that he bought from Craig is not my movie. Those were not the scenes from our movie. That was Craig taking idea that we had and trying to actually turn it into a script and make a real movie out of it that would sell. I don't think Don realizes it, but he didn't actually buy my movie. He bought Craig's script. I didn't even write that script. It's based on the short film. Let me just tell you, if you read that script that Don Murphy optioned, we didn't have half those locations! We had an apartment, a house, a bar, and the video store/bakery. That was all we had. That was an extrapolation from the short film, and that was all Craig's. So he didn't actually buy my little movie. He bought Craig's version of the script.

CRAIG HAMANN: Here's the deal: the first script was like eighteen pages. I wrote another draft that was thirty or forty. And then you have the full-length one now. The full-length one does contain things that I took off the set—things that Quentin wrote. It contains everything I could jam in there. There would not be a blueprint to shoot *My Best Friend's Birthday* if I hadn't written the very first script. As far as what we shot, I have to admit, Quentin is very fast on his feet. We had a lot of problems, which happens with all kinds of guerilla filmmaking. So could we shoot exactly what was in the script? No. We sometimes couldn't get the right locations. We sometimes couldn't get the right actors. Things would go wrong and we had to improvise, and Quentin was excellent at that. So sure, what you see and what we shot is different from the script. In some ways, sure, it deviates it from the script. But the blueprint is the screenplay. The forty-page script is what we had when we shot, and what you have now contains scenes that I wrote on my own. If Quentin feels that the screenplay is much different from what we shot, that's okay. I don't quite agree, but that's okay.

QUENTIN TARANTINO: Don Murphy trying to be a prick to me at that time was not a surprise. He went out of his way to be my enemy. The part that was heartbreaking about it had nothing to do with Don being a prick. The sad part about it was, Craig and I had no falling out, everything was fine between me and him, but we had grown a little more distant, a little more distant, a little more distant... But I still worked with Craig. He helped me out on a couple of things in post or on pre-production on a couple of the movies. He did some looping for me on *Reservoir Dogs* and he talked to Uma [Thurman] about heroin. It was really groovy that he helped us out that way.

As that was going on, me and Craig started trying to see each other again. So we'd go to a movie or go and get a couple of drinks and get to talking. We were just trying a little by little to get our friendship back. That process had started and then Craig sells Don Murphy *My Best Friend's Birthday*. He sells his rights to the script to the single biggest enemy I have in Hollywood! I was like, "*How can you do that? He's doing that just to fuck me! That's what he's doing. He paid you money to fuck me!*"

CRAIG HAMANN: I wish the whole thing with Don had not happened. I was in a situation where I needed money, and I needed it right away. And Don presented me with the opportunity of perhaps making some good money. I was willing to sell my part of *My Best Friend's Birthday*, but I was under the impression that Quentin would be approached to come in and be a part of what we were doing.

QUENTIN TARANTINO: Craig said, "Quentin, I promise you, Don said that's not what's coming out. He's not doing it for that reason. He loves the movie. He wants to make it." I said, "He's fucking lying to you. How can you talk to a guy like him and not realize you're being lied to? Knowing our history, how can you think that he means a word of that?" The deal was already done, so I said, "Okay, why don't you call up Don and ask him this or that or the other, since you're such good buddies with him." So Craig calls up Don and now that Don has the script, he told him to fuck off. And Craig knew I was right.

CRAIG HAMANN: When things got screwed up, I felt very bad. Did Quentin ask me to call Don and ask him some questions? I don't recall, but I can say this: in all the time I've known Don Murphy, and I do the like the guy, but...he's never done anything for me. He's never hired me for anything. The idea was, he was going do it as a film and I was going to be one of the writers. That was what was going to make me money, not the option. That's where the money was supposed to be. Also, I was not under the impression this was going be a big fuck-you to Quentin. I had no idea. I actually thought we would work together on this. I thought he'd just have a list of things he wanted to change and we'd change them. And he did have a list of those. He said he wanted the title changed. He wanted his name off of it. He wanted some character names changed. And I agreed to all of them. I was fine with it. All I wanted was a job writing the freaking script. That's all I was trying to do. I wasn't trying to hurt Quentin or hurt Don or anybody. This is kind of the reason she and I left the project. Once all the friction started, I realized this was just a big fuck you to Quentin and bailed out.

QUENTIN TARANTINO: I couldn't forgive Craig. He didn't betray me on purpose. He was fooled. But he shouldn't have been fooled. Don Murphy can't fool anybody about his intentions, but apparently he fooled Craig. I wasn't even mad at Craig; I was trying to build our friendship up again and this just kicked it right in the shit. I was just demoralized and sad that he would be such a sucker. I was just hurt and disappointed.

CRAIG HAMANN: I don't resent Quentin at all. There's no way that with all the stuff that came down that the side I was on couldn't have been partly at fault. There's no way any one person was just absolutely angelically perfect. Everybody made mistakes. I was in a bad situation financially, and I let that cloud my judgment. And I'm sorry that I did. I'm glad the film won't be remade. Sure, it would mean more money for me, and I could sure use it, but My Best Friend's Birthday is Quentin and I working together, period.

Despite their falling out, Hamann remains a fan and supporter of Tarantino's work and continues to hold out hope that things between the two friends can be made right again someday.

CRAIG HAMANN: After Quentin became successful, he moved on and made new friends, leaving all of us behind. Quentin once said he had to get out of Loserville in order to go forward and move ahead with his career. Maybe he felt we were all part of Loserville. Despite all of that, I'm very proud of all the things he's accomplished. I don't blame him for any of it. I just miss him.

If Quentin and I ran into each other somewhere, here's what I think would happen. I think we would be overjoyed to see one another. I think we would give each other a big hug and be very happy to see each other. I love the guy. I really do. I would love to see him again and clear the air. We don't have to see each other every day or be best buddies, but I would love to iron things out with him one day. I don't need anything from him or want anything, but I'd like to see him.

At some point in the early 2000s, rough footage from an uncorrected work print of *My Best Friend's Birthday* surfaced. It was comprised of odds and ends, a compilation of random scenes cobbled together.

ALAN SANBORN: Quentin, Rand, and myself all worked for Lewis Chesler, the producer of the series *The Hitchhiker*, at one time. Rand brought in a video copy of the rough-cut footage of *My Best Friend's Birthday* so I could see it. I said, "Can I get a copy of this?" And he said, "No! Absolutely not!" It was a big thing. "No copies of this can get out." It was top secret. That version was the same version that appears on the Internet today. I've been tempted at various times to go back and re-edit the scene I'm in because it's so rough.

LINDA KAYE: I was shown a videotape copy of it. It was scratchy. It was hard to hear. Since I was there for the filming, I was able to laugh and enjoy it. But somebody seeing it for the first time wouldn't have understood a thing. It didn't seem wonderful at all. I felt bad that Quentin was using it as a sort of calling card because I thought, Jesus, if you weren't there for the filming, you just wouldn't get the film.

Understandably, online reactions to the footage are mixed at best. One Internet Movie Database reviewer (using the moniker "twiggysmonkey") makes the improbable claim that the film "could have been Tarantino's best if it was completed." Another wildly praising comment was made on YouTube by a user named Jimmy the Gimmick, who lamented, "Imagine what Quentin could do if he remade this today. He could get the original cast, film on a better budget, rework the script a little bit. We could have another true blue classic." Other reviewers like "edwinharbor" recognize the film as the stepping stone it was: "QT's first film is a glimpse of what was to come from a very talented writer/director; rich banter with an entertaining and skewed look at life. Shot in black-and-white, on a very small budget, the film has many shortcomings compared to the director's other films." Then there are other reviewers, like Ryan Babbitt, who think it's a mess. "It's a really awful movie—largely due to the horrendous acting," writes Babbitt. "But what are you gonna do? It's essentially a student film for a man who was never a film student."

Rand Vossler says he reached out to Tarantino at one time regarding his possibly completing the film.

RAND VOSSLER: I contacted him and said, "I need a project. I need something to work on so I can get my head out of this negative place after things went south for me on *Natural Born Killers*. I would like to finish *My Best Friend's Birthday*. Would you give me your blessing?" And he was just like, "Nope."

It's tough because I know it's one of those things people would be interested in. I would like to see at least parts of it completed and put out there in a different form than the little half-inch video that circulates on the Internet now, which looks horrible. Because the actual footage looks really nice.

TODD HENSCHELL: It's sad what happened with *My Best Friend's Birthday*, because I think it could have been another *She's Gotta Have It*. It could have been one of those movies that were rough and didn't have any money, but it was freaking entertaining and it was funny. It's got a poignant story. Everybody worked hard on that, and I would like for everyone to be able to see it, even if my contribution was minimal. My participation has nothing to do with it. I would just like to see it because I think it should be out there.

Despite the film's untimely demise, *My Best Friend's Birthday* taught the future filmmakers many valuable lessons they would apply to their future endeavors. "That was one of my earliest film experiences," explains Avary. "I look at the making of that movie, even if it was unfinished, as having laid the foundation of an understanding of the basic principles of filmmaking."

QUENTIN TARANTINO: I learned a lot of lessons. Now I knew what it was like to look at a bunch of footage that you have and not be happy with it. So ultimately, it's more important to get footage that you're happy with than to get done in time. It's more important to get footage that you're proud of and can work with than just getting everybody home when they're supposed to go home. Nothing is more important than getting the footage you want to get. It's not doing the job, it's doing the job well, because the movie lasts forever. That was a huge lesson.

ROGER AVARY: Even though *My Best Friend's Birthday* is an unfinished film, it resulted in *Reservoir Dogs*. We were going to shoot that at Jerry Martinez's friend's motorcycle garage. It showed us that making a movie was expensive, and when you're making a movie with no budget like that, you have to coordinate a lot of stuff even though you can't pay anybody. You have to get everyone there and you have to make sure they're acting professional. This resulted in the idea of shooting in as few locations as possible, and with as few actors as possible. *Reservoir Dogs* utilizes the economy of trying to write engaging material in a single location.

Frankly, every movie I've done was a return to that exact same theory. I try to minimize the locations, make the story as interesting as possible, and go nuts within those values. That keeps the movie tight and cheap, allowing you to focus on what's important, which is the performances of the actor.

**Tarantino and Allen Garfield on the set of *My Best Friend's Birthday*.
(Courtesy of Todd Henschell)**

QUENTIN TARANTINO: Also, I learned that, okay, I don't want to make another movie for no money where everybody's working for free. I'm not down with that. I'm not good at that.

Clarence (Tarantino) selects a cake for Mickey's party. (Courtesy of Todd Henschell)

No matter what one does or does not believe regarding the quality of this little $5,000 movie, there can be no denying its legacy in having molded three screenwriter/directors in Tarantino, Avary, and Hamann.

It is in no way overstating the importance of *My Best Friend's Birthday* to say it played a tremendous role in shaping the filmmaker responsible for such classic films as *Pulp Fiction, Inglourious Basterds,* and *Django Unchained,* all of which were Academy Award nominees.

CRAIG HAMANN: When you look at the footage, you see that Quentin's signature was already starting to show. It wasn't there yet, and it shouldn't have been because he wasn't ready for it yet, but he was learning and his signature was starting to show. He was making something that was sort of half French farce and half Three Stooges.

I believe Quentin is extremely creative and talented. The thing that I like about his work is that he has a signature of his own. You know, Quentin has his own vision. Like his films or not, they belong to him. And he really truthfully is someone who loves films. I hear people talk about how much they love film, and this includes a lot of so-called filmmakers, but when push comes to shove, their movies look like everyone else's movies. If they love film so much, why didn't they get something out of it that ends up belonging to just them? Quentin does that. When he watches a movie, he takes part of it home with him in his soul. I've always admired that about him, and I always will.

QUENTIN TARANTINO: You know what I'm the proudest of regarding *My Best Friend's Birthday*? Look, this isn't just what I'm the most proud of in terms of this movie, it's the number one thing in life I'm most proud of. Of anything I've done, ever, this is the one thing I'm the most proud of... I worked for three years on this movie. It was my dream project. This was what I was going to do. And it ended up being nothing. Absolutely nothing! I gave my heart and soul for something for three years, and at the end of that three years I had nothing to show for it. Everybody else that I knew would have given up. Every single person I knew would have quit. At least as far as trying to be a director. The fact that I had such a failure and that I didn't give up—that I *persevered*—is the number one thing in my life that I'm the most proud of.

PART THREE

INTRODUCTION
DO YOU SEE THE SAME CAKE?
by Stephen Spignesi

My Best Friend's Birthday is to the films of Quentin Tarantino, what "Hello Little Girl" and "One after 909" are to the songs of The Beatles. Ur works. Just as the Beatles' tracks foreshadow future musical greatness, so does *My Best Friend's Birthday* foreshadow future marvelous Tarantino works, especially *True Romance*.

"Ur" means "primitive, original, earliest." So can we call *My Best Friend's Birthday* the "Ur *True Romance*"? Well, not really, but sort of. I suppose we can say it, if we want to confuse people who don't know what "ur" means, but there's definitely some merit in assigning that accolade to this short film.

As we know from the work done by this book's writer and editor Andy Rausch, *My Best Friend's Birthday* foreshadows Tarantino character names, lines of dialogue, plot contrivances, and even Tarantino's character Clarence Pool admitting he has a foot fetish. We've always known it about Tarantino, but the whole "life becomes art becomes life" mojo is fascinating and wryly amusing here, isn't it? "Wiggle your big toe," indeed.

My Best Friend's Birthday, Quentin Tarantino's first film, or what exists of it on film and viewable on YouTube, is an incredibly frugal production. What did it cost to make? $5,000 total? But the flick, such as it is, inexplicably, works. I wanted to know what happens after the last scene between Clarence and Misty. As evidence of Tarantino's genius, the film's paucity of production values quickly becomes irrelevant. The characters spring to life and the narrative grabs hold.

Personally, *My Best Friend's Birthday* will always have a warm spot in my heart if only because the character Mickey mentions Otis the town drunk from *The Andy Griffith Show*. My first book was *Mayberry*

My Home Town, an encyclopedia of, yes, *The Andy Griffith Show*. I'm a big fan, and Craig Hamann and Quentin may be as well. And adding to its appeal to me, later in the film, Bill Smith the baker talks about the Beatles album, *Sgt. Pepper's Lonely Hearts Club Band*. I've written three books about The Beatles. It's official: Quentin and Craig and I are soulmates. Well, at least creative pop culture kindred, right?

And speaking of pop culture, we've now come to expect a myriad of pop culture references in Tarantino's films. Flock of Seagulls is mentioned in *Pulp Fiction*. *Dirty Mary, Crazy Larry* appears in *Jackie Brown*. Paula Schulz from the Bob Crane movie *The Wicked Dreams of Paula Schulz* is referenced in *Kill Bill, Vol. 2*. "Stuck in the Middle with You" by Stealer's Wheel is played in *Reservoir Dogs*, which also has a lengthy deconstruction of Madonna's song, "Like a Virgin."

So it shouldn't surprise us that *My Best Friend's Birthday* has pop culture references, but what does surprise is the number of these nods in just thirty minutes of completed scenes. Tarantino and Hamann reference the following in the flick: Eddie Cochran, *The Partridge Family*, Elvis, *Godspell*, Marlon Brando, *A Countess from Hong Kong*, *The Wild One*, "Jailhouse Rock," *It Happened at the World's Fair*, *Dressed To Kill*, Brian De Palma, Nancy Allen, *The Legend of Hillbilly John*, *The Fury*, *The Patty Duke Show*, Rod Stewart, *GI Blues*, *Breathless*, Aldo Ray, The Big Bopper, "Chantilly Lace," *That Darn Cat*, *Squirm*, *The Evil That Men Do*, *Chato's Land*, *Rio Bravo*, *The Guinness Book of World Records*, Fred Astaire, Ginger Rogers, and *Miami Vice*.

One of my favorite scenes, and one of the funniest in the flick, is when Clarence wants to get Mickey a birthday cake. Clarence dictates a huge declamation to be written on Mickey's birthday cake: "Friendship will always be the love between Mickey and me, the joy of always knowing, our love is growing, because our friendship is showing..." The baker stops him and says, "Look at the size of the cake. Do you see the same cake?" Clarence then asks him what he *can* fit on the cake and the baker says, "Maybe 'Happy Birthday, Mickey.'" The "Do you see the same cake?" line is genius, frankly. I plan on using it when faced with obstinate supporters of non-evidence-based bullshit.

The karate fight scene with the mop is also pretty funny. And the "Your ass is grass and I'm the lawnmower" moment is *very Pulp Fiction/* Jules Winnfield-esque.

My Best Friend's Birthday is not easy to watch, primarily because we've all come to expect better quality...well, everything than what survived in the film. The lighting, sound, sets, etc. are rough-hewed, to say the least. But as I said earlier, none of that really plays too big a role in our appreciation of the film: as in all of QT's films, it's the characters that ensorcell us and keep us watching.

The following deconstruction of the film is a welcome addition to the body of work surrounding this lesser-known early effort of one of the world's greatest directors.

— STEPHEN SPIGNESI is a widely-published author and University of New Haven Practitioner in Residence (ret.) and writes extensively about popular culture and history. He is considered an authority on the work of Stephen King, The Beatles, Robin Williams, Woody Allen, *The Andy Griffith Show*, *ER*, and other pop culture subjects and TV shows.

SCRIPT AND FILM BREAKDOWN

Since the film was never completed, we're going to look at what exists of it, as well as the screenplay, scene by scene. This is the film that *My Best Friend's Birthday* might have been had it been finished. While the long-form script is about half Tarantino with the other half being written solely by Hamann, this is as close as we can possibly come to seeing what a full-length version of the film might have looked like. Naturally this isn't an exact science, but it's literally the best that's possible.

> *The following story takes place in Torrance, California. Almost nothing ever happens in Torrance, but sometimes a person has a bad night there.*
> —"Special Note" from the screenplay

The first scene begins with a Ford Mustang driving down the street in Torrance, California.

CRAIG HAMANN: I'm a big Mustang fanatic. We had to have a car. I thought of a friend of ours named Ron Amick who had a built '67 Mustang. I thought maybe he'd let us use it, which he probably would have had this scene been shot, because he's a very nice guy. That's why that came up. I think if you look in all my scripts, you'll find a Ford Mustang somewhere.

The Mustang is being driven by Mickey Burnett (Hamann). As he's driving, he's listening to his best friend and coworker Clarence Pool (Tarantino), a deejay on the radio. The rockabilly station both Clarence and Mickey work for is called K-Billy (KBLI).

CRAIG HAMANN: Part of the reason Quentin chooses the name Clarence a lot is because he likes the name. And it's a good name. It has a lot of character in it. With Mickey, part of that is because Quentin thought I looked like a Mickey. The last name, Burnett, came from Sonny Crockett's alter ego Sonny Burnett on *Miami Vice*. We were after rockabilly, and we both thought that sounded like a rockabilly name. And Clarence Pool? Same thing. These just sounded like good names for these guys to have. I think the name Clarence Pool really fit Quentin's look at the time, because he had this great big pompadour.

As Mickey listens, Clarence tells listeners that his radio show will be followed by Mickey's. He then announces that today is Mickey's birthday. Mickey speaks aloud to the radio, saying he doesn't want Clarence to say how old he is, so naturally Clarence does just that, informing everyone that Mickey is thirty years old today, even though his birthday is actually the following day.

CRAIG HAMANN: Quentin and I, there's a huge difference in our ages. I was a little over thirty, and Quentin was under thirty. Realistically, looking at it on film, I looked thirty. I wasn't that far over thirty. I can't remember exactly what I was at the time. But it was an age set we felt we looked like, so that's why we went with it.

When I first started, I think having them work together might've been an idea that Quentin and I came up with together. We actually had Mickey working at Garage-Doors-R-Us, which we made up. We eventually shifted over, deciding to have Mickey work at the same place as Clarence. So we ended up having him work at K-Billy, which was nice because we had the whole rockabilly music theme going. Quentin as Clarence had the whole rockabilly thing. So it worked a little better that way. I think the K-Billy name might have been my idea, but I'm not so sure where the idea to have a very small rockabilly station originally came from. I think we came up with that together. I think Quentin had a lot to do with that, because of the rockabilly influence.

To commemorate Mickey's thirtieth birthday, Clarence dedicates thirty minutes of nonstop rockabilly to him. He also encourages older listeners to call in on Mickey's show and share what they did on their own thirtieth birthdays. Mickey is annoyed by this and switches off the radio.

The next scene is inside KBLI, where Clarence, described as a "rockabilly boy" and a "hillbilly cat," is about to interview an on-air guest named Lenny Otis (Rowland Wafford) on his aptly-titled "The Clarence Pool Show." But first Clarence takes a phone call from a listener asking to make a request. Clarence shows himself to be an arrogant ass here, informing the listener that he doesn't take requests, unlike other deejays, because he's Clarence Pool and he does whatever he wants. Why is this, you ask? Because Clarence says his tastes are so respected that he's allowed to do whatever he likes. He then calls the listener "dickbait" and hangs up on him.

CRAIG HAMANN: The whole Clarence character, from beginning to end, he's smug. Not because he's a prick as much as he's so into being cool. And his definition of coolness is straight ahead from Elvis Presley and rockabilly music. He has this attitude through the whole movie like he's got his shit together and he knows what he's doing. But he doesn't, and that's part of the joke.

When the interview begins, we learn that Lenny Otis is the president of the California chapter of the Eddie Cochran Fan Club.

In this scene Tarantino uses one of the oldest tricks in the low-budget filmmaking handbook: in an attempt to conceal what is obviously a makeshift set in someone's house or apartment that in no way resembles an actual radio station booth, Tarantino and company attempt to mask the backdrop by draping something across the wall. In this case it's a huge American flag, which looks pretty cool behind Tarantino and Wafford, even if it doesn't look like a radio station. This trick has been done throughout film history. Notorious schlockmeister Ed Wood would often drape a sheet across a wall in his films to conceal what were obviously the insides of someone's home in films like *Plan 9 from Outer Space* to fake interiors of airplane cockpits and spacecraft. It goes without saying that the *My Best Friend's Birthday* crew manages to achieve a suspension of disbelief that is far more effective than anything Wood ever could. "All of *My Best Friend's Birthday* was shot on locations," says Hamann.

"We had to dress the backgrounds the best we could within a short time."

The walls are adorned with movie posters and photos of musicians and actors, such as Marlon Brando in *The Wild One*. One poster is for *The Legend of Hillbilly John*, which is a movie about a rockabilly boy who meets the devil. Then there is, of course, a poster for *The Fury*, a film from Tarantino's favorite director Brian De Palma.

As an actor, Tarantino chews through the scenery a bit here, his style manic and hyperactive, causing one to reflect on the various people in this book who describe him as being like an anxious puppy. But his work is effective, and he delivers some great monologues in the radio scenes. As would become a signature of his work, he utilizes a lot of long, unbroken shots.

While the interview happens, Mickey enters the radio station in another part of the building. He is greeted by a secretary named Nutmeg (Alan Sanborn), who first insults Mickey for being old and turning thirty and then talks him into covering for him while he goes to get a pizza (from "Drooley's Pizza"). Nutmeg takes off to get the pizza, and Mickey sits at his desk.

Once again what is obviously a room inside an apartment or house stands in for a radio station reception office. This is in no way a knock against the filmmakers. When shooting a no-budget film, filmmakers are forced to use and make the best of whatever locations they can get. Tarantino and Hamann's script is engaging enough that the audience pays close attention to the characters speaking, effectively distracting from the makeshift sets.

The station owner, Mr. Trumper, walks in and informs Mickey that the station's biggest contributor, an elderly woman known as "Grandma Mohmmi" will be coming for a visit. He tells Mickey to be extremely nice to her, and also asks him to instruct Clarence to play more live Las Vegas recordings of Elvis Presley, as those are Grandma Mohmmi's favorites. Mickey explains that Clarence doesn't like to play the later-years Elvis songs, instead preferring to play his younger rockabilly stuff. Trumper cuts him off and tells him Clarence is to play more of the Vegas material, and that's it. Trumper then leaves.

Clancy (Stevo Polyi), another deejay, walks into the reception area, sitting down on the desk. (Here it's apparent that the fictitious radio station has a similar atmosphere and attitude to that of Video Archives, where Tarantino worked. Similar to the video store, the KBLI employees hang around, even when they're not working.) Clancy makes a crack about Mickey's old age (everyone in this script is apparently really young, because thirty is universally seen as being decrepit). Clancy brings up another sore subject—Mickey's ex-girlfriend Pandora, who has just left him. Mickey tells him he doesn't want to talk about either of these subjects.

Clancy then reveals himself to be a prankster, handing Mickey a piece of garlic-flavored gum. Mickey, not realizing its gag gum, pops it into his mouth just as the phone rings. He answers it and it's Grandma Mohmmi. In the middle of his conversation with her, Mickey realizes something is amiss with the gum. He blurts out "*Shit!*," and turns to Clancy, cursing at him and calling him names. Mickey momentarily forgets about the phone call and listens to Clancy talk about going into a novelty shop and purchasing $50 worth of gag items. One of these items is a bag of itching powder. Unable to get the taste out of his mouth, Mickey screams more obscenities. He then remembers that Grandma Mohmmi is on the phone. He picks up the phone and tries to apologize, but finds that she has hung up, believing Mickey was screaming at her.

CRAIG HAMANN: Names like Unruly Julie or Grandma Mohmmi were good examples of Quentin coming up with some funny names and funny characters that you never really meet. That's part of Quentin's brilliance.

It should be noted that this description of events describes the screenplay, rather than the film itself. The slight difference in the film is that the conversation and scenario take place entirely between Clancy and Nutmeg, rather than Clancy and Mickey. (Hamann says this decision was Tarantino's, but he no longer remembers the reason for it.)

The story returns to Clarence interviewing Lenny Otis. They discuss the day Eddie Cochran died. Lenny doesn't remember it because he wasn't born yet. Clarence then explains a day when he was only three years old and was feeling blue:

CLARENCE: There was this one particular day. I felt really depressed. For no reason whatsoever. I had no idea why, but I was feelin' low. I even thought of suicide. I was gonna get in the bathtub and slit my wrists with a razor blade. I was actually gonna do it. Now for a three-year-old to be thinkin' like this, you gotta be feelin' pretty bad. The only reason I didn't do it was *The Partridge Family* was about ready to come on, and I wanted to see it. So I thought I'd watch that, and do it after the show was over. But *The Partridge Family* was really funny that night and after the show I was feelin' better. So, I didn't do it.

Clarence explains that he later learned the day he'd been depressed was the day Eddie Cochran died. The story is silly and nonsensical, which is the point, and the monologue is classic Tarantino, complete with the pop culture references that were a trademark of his early work.

BRENDA HILLHOUSE: It's funny, but when I watched the scene with him in the radio station talking to the guy—that's Quentin. That's completely him. And you know, I think that's one of the best scenes I've ever seen him do. And the things his character is saying are things that are really from his heart. That dialogue was about the things that appealed to him in real life.

As Clarence and Lenny continue talking about the fallen rock singer and the California chapter of his fan club, Mickey and Clancy discuss the baggie of itching powder Clancy purchased for Clarence. Mickey then goes to the recording booth, where, in a demonstration of their friendship, he and Clarence sing the theme song to *The Patty Duke Show*—just because. Clarence introduces Mickey and Lenny. Mickey hands the baggie of powder to Clarence, who mistakes it for cocaine. Mickey leaves, returning to the front office.

Clarence asks Lenny if he's cool, to which Lenny responds that he is. "Good," says Clarence, pouring the powder out on the counter and cutting lines with a razor blade. Clarence offers some to Lenny, who declines. Clarence then snorts two rails—one in each nostril—as the song ends. He turns to Lenny and asks him what first made him interested in Eddie Cochran. Lenny is stunned at finally having an opportunity to speak; until now Clarence has completely dominated their conversation. Lenny starts to talk about how he first heard Cochran singing "Pink Legged Slacks." As this is happening, Clarence realizes something is wrong. He attempts to blow his nose. Now in pain, he bangs his fists on the counter. Clarence screams that he's in hell. He flails around, pointing at the phone and repeatedly saying "911." Nutmeg is walking past the recording booth carrying his pizza box. When he sees what's happening to Clarence, he runs to get Mickey.

When Mickey and Nutmeg arrive at the recording booth, followed by Mr. Trumper, they find Clarence lying on the floor, kicking and screaming. Mickey asks the startled Lenny what happened, and Lenny tells him.

CRAIG HAMANN: I think it's one of the funniest scenes we have in the movie. That is completely Quentin, 100 percent. He wrote it and directed it, and did a hell of a good job with it. The whole thing with the itching powder, that was Quentin. There's been some pieces between it where Mickey and Clarence are talking, which I wrote, but the Clarence stuff, everything they're talking about there, that's all Quentin. And the whole idea of him snorting the itching powder, that was Quentin, too.

There's a part in there where Clarence is rubbing his nose, and he's going crazy, and he screams, "*I am in hell!*" That's actually from Mel Gibson's character in the movie *Gallipoli*. He screams, "I am in hell!," and we all liked that. Quentin incorporated that, knowing that Mel Gibson's character is very serious, and in this, it's very funny. That's where it came from. It was an inside joke between some of us working on the film. Scott McGill, Quentin, and myself in particular, got a big kick out of it because we knew where it came from.

Stevo Polyi played Clancy. The thing I remember about Stevo, besides the fact he was a very likable guy, a very funny guy, was that he just had good energy around him. He made me laugh. He had this great smile and he used to say things that were off the wall, and deliberately so. He was perfect for the character Clancy, in the sense that I could see Stevo going out and getting itching powder and thinking, "This is going to be fun. I'm going to prank some people." Stevo handled that scene pretty well. I thought it was funny.

The next scene takes place in the evening at Mickey's apartment. He arrives home to find his ex-girlfriend Pandora (Linda Kaye) inside, holding a record. Mickey is excited to see her, mistakenly thinking she has come back to him after their breakup. He kisses her and even lifts her off the ground, hugging her.

> MICKEY: This might turn out to be a good birthday after— Whoa! Is that why you came back today? You remembered my birthday?

Mickey inevitably has his heart broken all over again when Pandora nonchalantly informs him she only came to retrieve a Rod Stewart album she left behind. (It might be noted that in addition to Pandora mentioning Rod Stewart, there's an additional musical pop culture reference here as there is a visible Elvis Presley *GI Blues* LP decoratively standing upright. Pandora also mentions Presley (mispronouncing his name as Prest-ley.) Before Mickey can respond, he hears the sound of the toilet flushing. Oliver (Rich Turner), a well-groomed yuppie (the antithesis of Clarence and Mickey) walks out of the bathroom, announcing that he's just taken a dump. Mickey asks Pandora how she got into his apartment, remembering that he had taken her key back at the time of their breakup. Pandora tells him that Oliver broke in. Pandora then explains that Oliver is an actor, like her, and that she met him during a Torrance Community Theatre production of *Godspell*, in which he plays Jesus.

As Pandora and Oliver leave, Pandora, oblivious to Mickey's pain, tells him to call her sometime to catch up. (It might be noted that here is a *Breathless* poster next to the door. As discussed elsewhere in this book, Tarantino was a huge fan of the Richard Gere film.) Outside, Mickey hears Oliver ask Pandora if she and Mickey used to "have a scene." Pandora downplays Mickey's importance in her life, saying, "Just a little one."

CRAIG HAMANN: Pandora was played by Linda Kaye. I didn't know Linda very well. I think she and Quentin might have dated at one time. They certainly were good friends. We met that night. Quentin rehearsed us. That scene, I'd say that eighty to ninety percent of it is Quentin's, in terms of writing. It was an interesting scene in that I was trying to be very understanding as Mickey. I couldn't believe what I was seeing with Pandora and this Oliver guy, who was played by Rich Turner, a very fine actor.

Mickey's just sitting there because Pandora's come back to him, but in fact she hasn't; she just wants to get her Rod Stewart album. Oliver says something really tacky at the end. "I see you like Elvis, my aunt likes Elvis." It really is just one big kick in the balls to Mickey.

Mickey is sitting there, feeling melancholy. This onset of depression is interrupted by Clarence, who barges in with a half-empty beer in his hand. Clarence goes on a rant, revealing that both he and Mickey have been fired because of Clarence's snorting the itching powder. Clarence rants about the number of disc jockeys who are stoned when they're on the air.

> CLARENCE: We made that station. The original cool cat Clarence Pool and Midnight Mickey were K-Billy. We were the gurus of rockabilly airwaves, I'll tell ya that.

Clarence suggests they should establish their own radio station, theorizing that no one would want to listen to K-Billy once they learned that Clarence and Mickey were gone. In mid-rant, Clarence decides they will sue for wrongful termination and then use the money to start their own station. Then, finally, Clarence realizes Mickey isn't speaking. He asks what's wrong, to which Mickey says he got fired, he's turning thirty, and Pandora stopped by to hurt him again.

CRAIG HAMANN: After Pandora and Oliver leave, the rest of the writing in that scene is mine. It's mostly just Clarence coming in and venting about being fired. I wrote a lot of dialogue for Quentin in that. He really liked what I wrote for him. The exchange between Mickey and Clarence for the rest of the scene, which goes on for a while, that was my writing. I have dialogue in that scene, but I really wrote it more for Quentin. I really wanted him to come in there and have a really cool moment, and have it be with Mickey, and not just by himself. I love that Quentin pulled it off really well and did a good job. And again, we didn't know what we were doing, so we were doing the best we could. I love that he came in and he's saying, "My point is life's cool, we're cool, life goes on, fuck everything else." I just thought that was perfect for Quentin as an actor, and I thought it would be good material that was well suited for him. And sure enough, he did a great job.

After talking about a girl named Cecilia (Leanne Chambers) that he's been seeing—a girl with a boyfriend—Clarence tries to console Mickey. He decides they'll throw a party for Mickey's birthday. Mickey keeps trying to tell Clarence his birthday isn't actually until the following day, but Clarence won't listen. Clarence decides he wants to get Mickey laid for his birthday. Mickey tells him he's tired, but Clarence won't hear of it, insisting that this will be an epic night. Mickey tells Clarence he's just going to stay home and go to bed. Clarence tries to object, but Mickey closes the door.

From Mickey's place, Clarence goes to Ronny's Bar, which the script describes as being a dive bar. Ronny (Ronald Coleman) is the owner and bartender. When Clarence enters the place, Ronny is listening to music Clarence doesn't approve of. This leads Clarence to unplug the radio. When Ronny asks why they can't listen to his music, Clarence tells him it's because his music sucks.

CRAIG HAMANN: Ronald Coleman was really good at portraying strength through weakness. Kind of act like a big shot, when you're really not. Quentin and I designed all that for Ronny as the bartender. I wrote a lot of the dialogue, but Quentin certainly added a lot to it. It was kind of a fifty/fifty thing. One of the things about Ronny is, he's the type of guy, when he delivered dialogue, he was almost lying when he was delivering it. I don't mean that in a bad way. It was a good way. It made it very funny.

In the beginning, when they're talking, Ronny's going, "Come on, Clarence, why can't we listen to my kind of music? Give me one good reason!" Clarence goes, "One good reason? Because your music sucks." That's just perfect Ronny and Quentin. I mean, Ronny and Quentin knew each other. We all knew each other from the James Best Theater Center. That's where we first met Ronny. That's where we started seeing his work, and that's where we became friends with him. He was a really nice guy.

Clarence goes to the jukebox and plays several songs, including Johnny Cash's "Ring of Fire." After making his selections, he sees a shapely young woman named Misty Knight (Crystal Shaw) playing pool.

CRAIG HAMANN: Both Quentin and I enjoyed working with Crystal. She worked really, really hard. She tried very hard in this. It was a good role for her. The character Misty was designed for Crystal because that's kind of the way she is—not a hooker, but very upbeat about things. Very sweet. She was good-looking, an old girlfriend of mine. A good friend of both Quentin's and mine. We asked her to play Misty and she was there through most of the shoot.

QUENTIN TARANTINO: I actually think Crystal Shaw gives the best performance in the movie. She should be proud of it. I think she's really good in it. She worked so hard for me, and she was such a lovely person. She really gave her all and always supported me in a big way.

Thinking Misty might be a woman he can set Mickey up with, Clarence approaches her as she plays pool. She doesn't see Clarence behind her. She rears back to shoot, inadvertently poking him in the eye with her pool stick. Misty apologizes and the two engage in the usual mindless boring get-to-know-you chit-chat (and yes, that's a *Pulp Fiction* reference). In the course of the conversation Misty reveals herself to be a fan of both rockabilly music and Clarence's now-defunct radio show. Clarence then recruits Misty to be Mickey's date for the evening. When it becomes clear that

Clarence wants Misty to sleep with Mickey, she reveals that she's a call girl.

> MISTY: I should explain that I'm not a hooker, I'm a call girl. Call girls are much more classier.

Alabama Worley will make a similar assertion in Tarantino's later screenplay for *True Romance*. It might also be noted that a male character becoming romantically involved (and not just a customer) with a call girl occurs in both films, as well as the Tarantino-produced Roger Avary film *Killing Zoe*.

Clarence and Misty haggle over money. Misty says she'll do it for $50, but Clarence counters with thirty. They ultimately compromise and settle on forty. Clarence gives her the money and a key to Mickey's place. He instructs her to go to Mickey's apartment and entertain him. Then, afterwards, she is to bring him over to Clarence's so they can all party.

CRAIG HAMANN: We liked the idea that Misty was anything but an experienced hooker. She was extremely inexperienced.

After talking briefly with Ronny, Clarence leaves. Moments later, Misty's pimp, a black man named Clifford (Al Harrell) walks in. Clifford is decidedly un-pimp-like, dressed in an outdated and unkempt suit. The screenplay describes Clifford as speaking in a monotone manner.

CRAIG HAMANN: We had Al Harrell playing the pimp. Al, in our movie and in real life, was not driving at that time. He had no license and he had no car. We used that in the movie so that Misty's pimp didn't even have a car. He's taking the bus, which we thought would be pretty funny. And Al could relate to that. Al and Crystal got along very well also.

Clifford was the name of somebody Al knew in real life. I don't know if Al liked him or not, but Quentin liked the name, particularly for someone who's supposed to be a pimp, because that name doesn't fit what you expect a pimp's name to sound like. Everything about this pimp is wrong. *Everything*. His suit is

Clifford the Pimp (Al Harrell) talks to a character played by Richard "Rick" Squeri. (Courtesy of Todd Henschell)

wrong. His tie is wrong. The fact that he doesn't have a car. The fact that he probably doesn't have anyone else he's pimping besides Misty, who's never been a hooker before. She doesn't know what she's doing and neither does Clifford.

Adding to this, you've got Al playing the role so dryly, which is great. That's exactly what we wanted. Quentin rehearsed him to do that, and it was terrific.

Clifford (another name Tarantino later recycled in *True Romance*) is looking for Misty. Clifford asks Ronny where she went, but he says he won't tell. When Clifford snatches Ronny by his collar and threatens him, Ronny changes his mind, giving him the address to Clarence's apartment. (His apartment building is located on Carpenter Street, and the apartment number is thirteen—a reference to John Carpenter's *Assault on Precinct 13*.) Ronny finally speaks up, but only after the pimp has left. He mutters, "He better hope our paths never cross again."

In the next scene, we see Clarence at Bill Smith's Video Bakery, which is a combination video store and bakery. (Both the wrongness of Clifford's pimp character and the ludicrousness of a video/bakery hybrid are two of the best examples of the artistic absurdity that make *My Best Friend's Birthday* unique.)

CRAIG HAMANN: That name came from William Smith, who was one of Quentin's favorite actors. He had a fascination and admiration for William Smith. We both felt that way, but especially Quentin. So it became Bill Smith's Video Bakery, which we thought would be interesting. Some of that also had to do with the fact that we didn't have the money and the time to properly recreate a bakery. We shot that at Video Archives, so we just threw in that it was a video store as well as a bakery.

Clarence is talking to the business' proprietor, Bill Smith (Allen Garfield). Clarence orders a cake for Mickey's party. As they discuss Mickey and his recent problems, Bill brings up an ongoing argument he and Clarence have about the films of Elvis Presley. This is natural, right? Who doesn't argue about Elvis movies when they visit a bakery? When Bill questions Elvis' acting chops, Clarence gives a long-winded, brilliant monologue about the merits of thespian Elvis.

CLARENCE: When you say Elvis was shitty, you're probably talkin' about the Elvis who was in *Girls, Girls,*

Clarence (Tarantino) and Bill Smith (Allen Garfield) appear together in a largely-improvised scene in which they discuss the merits of Elvis Presley as an actor. (Courtesy of Todd Henschell)

Girls, Harem Scarum, Kissin' Cousins, or *Paradise, Hawaiian Style.* That's not what I'm talkin' about. Not to say he was bad in those. He was as good as a person can be in *Clambake.* But what I'm talkin' about is the first movies he made, like *Jailhouse Rock*—which is one of Mickey's all-time favorites—*Lovin' You, King Creole, Flaming Star.* He was so natural, so sexy, so Elvis.

CRAIG HAMANN: Quentin wrote the great dialogue that we find later in some of his other work, about Elvis and about how he felt about him. He has this argument with Bill, who was played by Allen Garfield. Quentin had dialogue in there that was Clarence saying Elvis was a great actor, he just made some shitty movies, which Quentin really felt. Then Allen goes, "Wait a minute, Elvis isn't a great actor, these other guys are great actors." That was very Allen Garfield-esque, written specifically for him, and probably written because that's how Allen felt.

A lot of that dialogue is Quentin's. I added a little bit to it, but Allen and Quentin ad-libbed a lot. Allen was all over the map with the dialogue.

This scene was brilliantly shot in regards to overcoming situational obstacles, with the camera shooting the actors from below, managing to conceal that the scene was shot inside a video store. Tarantino and Allen Garfield had some minor disagreements while filming the scene, and those exchanges may have fueled the fictitious argument that takes place on screen, providing the scene with an added degree of realism.

Bill asks Clarence what he wants written on Mickey's cake. Clarence then begins to rattle off a poetic message as long as his Elvis monologue was (the quote was just an excerpt).

CRAIG HAMANN: The poem for the top of the cake was mine. I came up with it. It was kind of a friendship thing between Quentin and me at the time. It's such a corny and ridiculous poem, too.

Bill informs Clarence that he can't fit all that on a cake. (He uses the line, "Time out, Green Bay," which will later be recycled in *Reservoir Dogs*.)

BILL: I got about enough room for "Happy birthday, Mickey."

CLARENCE: Aww, man. Everyone puts that on their cake.

BILL: Everyone named Mickey.

Finally, Clarence agrees to go with something simple and proceeds to purchase a plethora of sweets, including cookies, chocolate eclairs, doughnuts, turnovers, apple fritters, and pie for the party.

The story cuts to Clifford walking down a dark street, angrily spouting lines that are similar to the *Superfly TNT/Guns of the Navarone* speech Jules Winnfield says after Vincent Vega has "shot Marvin in the face" in *Pulp Fiction*.

CLIFFORD: I'm a hand grenade with the pin pulled. I'm a fuming volcano of rage ready to erupt.

Back at Mickey's apartment, Mickey is standing in the shower, depressed. Suddenly, the curtain is pulled back and Misty is standing there. Mickey screams, startled. An exuberant Misty explains who she is and informs him that she's his birthday surprise. She then sings "Happy Birthday" as he stands there naked with the water running. Mickey doesn't say anything, so Misty tells him she will be waiting in the next room. Once he's finished his shower, they can start the party. She finishes by telling him she loves his radio show, and then she turns and leaves. Mickey stands there, stunned and confused. Misty opens the bathroom door again, telling him, "Keep it casual. What you have on is fine."

Much has been made of the fact that something extreme happens each of the three times Vincent goes to the restroom in *Pulp Fiction*. A similar thing occurs in *My Best Friend's Birthday* each of the three times Mickey takes a shower. Here it isn't violence like it is in *Pulp*, but it's still a significant event.

In the next scene we see Clarence in his apartment, trying to call Mickey. He's standing beside a table holding a variety of goodies for the party, including cake, doughnuts, ice cream, and punch. Clarence gets a busy signal. He calls the operator and tells her he needs to place an emergency call.

We then see Cecilia, the woman Clarence is seeing—a female cop with a macho cop boyfriend. She's sitting on her bed, dressed in her uniform, talking on the phone to her analyst, Dr. Reighold, voiced by Tarantino. (It should be noted that Tarantino later used a variation of this name for another doctor—Dr. Emil Reingold—in his *Natural Born Killers* script.) Cecilia is discussing her quandary in choosing between her two lovers, Clarence and Eddie (David O'Hara), who is also her police partner. There is one particularly funny line here where she says that Clarence is cool, or "at least he tells me he is."

While they're discussing this, an operator cuts into the line and announces that she has an emergency call from Aldo Ray. (This is a nod to actor Aldo Ray, whom Tarantino has said was the inspiration for *Pulp Fiction* character Butch's appearance. Tarantino also gave a nod to the actor through the name Aldo Raine in *Inglourious Basterds*.)

Dr. Reighold says, "You never told me you knew Aldo Ray." Cecilia tells him she doesn't and that she will call him back.

CRAIG HAMANN: I wrote the majority of this scene, but Quentin added some things. All the Aldo Ray stuff was Quentin's, without a doubt.

Cecilia speaks to Clarence, who greets her with an impression of the Big Bopper from "Chantilly Lace" saying, "*Hello, baaaaaabbbb-byyyy!*"

Clarence invites her to a surprise party for Mickey. He says the party will consist of just the four of them—Clarence, Cecilia, Mickey, and Misty. Cecilia keeps trying to tell him she's worried that her boyfriend Eddie knows she's been cheating, but he pays her no mind. When she tells him that Eddie is very strong and very jealous, he tells her that Eddie better not mess with him. (As all this occurs in the few minutes of edited footage, it is intercut with cutaway shots of Eddie lifting weights, as well as aiming a gun at the screen, dressed as a cop, ordering, "*Freeze, faggot!*") As Clarence tries to convince Cecilia to continue seeing him, she hangs up.

Although it's become popular in film circles to knock Tarantino's acting, which is actually quite good in *From Dusk Till Dawn*, he's not bad in the existing scenes from *My Best Friend's Birthday*. This scene, however, is the exception. For some reason he employs a strange "tough guy" affectation—the stereotypical "goomba" Italian accent that appears in low-rent mob flicks—that he doesn't use in the rest of the film. When he's basically just being a variation of himself in other scenes, he's far more effective.

Back at Mickey's apartment, Misty is lying on the couch, waiting for Mickey. The scene begins with the camera slowly panning up Misty's body, starting with her feet. (Not only does this reference Tarantino's well-documented foot fetish, but is a similar shot to those of Bridget Fonda in *Jackie Brown* and Sidney Poitier in *Death Proof* [2007].) Suddenly, Clifford bursts through the door. He becomes enraged because Misty has secured her own customer, and the two of them argue.

CRAIG HAMANN: You get these great moments between Misty

Mickey (Craig Hamann) punches Clifford (Al Harrell). (Courtesy of Todd Henschell)

and Clifford where they're arguing. Clifford will say something like, "I came all the way down here on the bus..." And he does this in a very dry "I don't know what the hell I'm doing" way. That's what we were shooting for. We weren't taking any stabs at anybody. We weren't taking stabs at blacks, or pimps, or hookers, or anything like that. This is just part of a really crazy world that we have in this script, that took place in Torrance, California, of all places. We just wanted everybody in this movie to be a real character.

Misty fires Clifford from being her pimp after mocking him for not being able to afford a car. Clifford approaches her and starts choking her, and she accidentally punches him in the nose, injuring him. Clifford angrily throws Misty to the floor.

Mickey walks in, having no idea Clifford is there. Mickey sees what's happening and demands that the pimp leave. This angers Clifford, who then produces a pair of nunchaku ("numchucks")

Clifford (Al Harrell) assumes the *Karate Kid* crane kick position.
(Courtesy of Todd Henschell)

Tarantino, Al Harrell, Rick Squeri, and Craig Hamann work out the scene in which Harrell's character goes into the trash can. (Courtesy of Todd Henschell)

from his suit jacket. He begins twirling them maniacally. He charges at Mickey, but Mickey runs into the bathroom, closing the door. Clifford's momentum propels him forward, and he crashes into the door, injuring himself, and he falls down. Mickey steps out. He picks up Clifford and attempts to drag him to the door to throw him out, but Clifford breaks free. He lets out a Bruce Lee "karate scream" and moves into a comical praying mantis stance like Daniel in *The Karate Kid*. The two engage in a ridiculous fight played for laughs, with Clifford brandishing a mop, using its handle as if it's a fighting staff. Eventually, Mickey punches Clifford so hard he flies back and falls out the window, headfirst into a trash can.

TODD HENSCHELL: I gave Al a lot of crap when he was in that garbage can. I said, "How are you doing in there, Al?"

Mickey runs to his Mustang, but finds that it won't start, which is very much in keeping with the day he's had. As he's inside the car attempting to start it, a ten-year-old girl on roller skates approaches, knocking on the window. Mickey rolls the window down. In a comical exchange, the girl knows who he is and comments about Pandora having left him. The conversation becomes even more humorous when the little girl then accuses Mickey of trying to seduce her, eventually skating away and yelling at the top of her lungs that "Midnight Mickey is a sickie."

Clarence is driving down the street by Mickey's apartment building and sees Misty standing in the street. Misty climbs into Clarence's car and says she's ready to leave. She then suggests that she and Clarence hook up and have their own party since their respective dates have fallen through.

In the next scene, we see Cecilia's boyfriend Eddie visiting the office of a private investigator named Arno Posner (as this scene was never filmed, no one was cast for the role). Arno is sitting behind a desk drinking a can of beer. Eddie is immediately established as an aggressive jerk. He demands that Arno show him surveillance photos he shot of Cecilia and Clarence at the Dew Drop Motel (a reference to the Little Richard song "Dew Drop Inn"). Eddie becomes enraged and punches a file cabinet. He then attacks the private investigator. He asks Arno what Clarence's name is, and Arno tells him, providing him his contact information as well. Eddie stalks out.

CRAIG HAMANN: I'm not sure where the name Posner came from. That might have been Quentin's, but I know Arno was my contribution. The idea to make it the Dew Drop Motel was Quentin's idea.

We wrote this whole private investigator thing because we wanted Eddie to have a reason to be jealous. But we also had it because we wanted to reveal that Eddie has an extreme temper. He punches a file cabinet, kicks a trash can, and just basically beats the shit out of Arno's office.

Eddie goes to a pay phone to call Clarence, but doesn't have change. He sees a young man sitting outside playing guitar. Eddie accosts him and steals his change, calling him a "welfare wimp" before returning to the phone booth. Eddie calls and reaches Clarence's answering machine, which plays rockabilly music and features Clarence once again mimicking the Big Bopper saying *"Hello, baaaaby!"* and trying to act cool. There is another monologue here that reminds us

how cool Clarence believes he is.
Eddie leaves his own message:

> EDDIE: You asshole! This is Eddie. I hope you know who I am. I hope that name means somethin' to you. I'm the man who's gonna drop-kick you to hell! Cecilia's my woman. She's my property, and you been messin' with her. Look, garbage can, when I find you and when I lay my hands on you, I'm gonna punch a hole through your rockabilly face! Then I'm gonna body-slam your rockabilly carcass to the ground! Then tie your rockabilly ass to the back of my car, and drag you down the middle of the street. I just wanted you to know that. *I'm on my way!*

CRAIG HAMANN: This was another scene where we were both writing. There's the voice-over on the machine, and that's Quentin's writing. But then there's Eddie's response, which was part Quentin's and part mine. I really like the whole thing about Eddie planning to find Clarence and tie him to his car and drag him around. It shows what Eddie is like. We felt it was important to kind of establish how nasty Eddie was in these scenes, and to kind of build up the whole thing before they meet.

We are then treated to an inordinately long unbroken shot (lasting a full minute) of the answering machine as both Clarence's message and then Eddie's play. At the end of this, the camera pans up and we see Clarence and Misty entering the apartment, arm-in-arm. Clarence tries to impress Misty, telling her about his outlandish plans to open a Rockabilly Burger chain with Mickey that will feature things like the Be Bopalula Burger and the Breathless Burrito. (Early precursors to Tarantino's legendary *Pulp Fiction* creation, the Big Kahuna Burger.)

CRAIG HAMANN: This dialogue came from Quentin's wanting to open his own '50s restaurant. Of course, the Breathless Burrito is a reference to *Breathless*—the one with Richard Gere—because Quentin loved that movie.

It should also be noted that Tarantino's idea for a "'50s restaurant" would later come to life (again in *Pulp Fiction*) as Jack Rabbit Slim's.

The walls of Clarence's apartment are covered with film posters that belonged to Tarantino himself, including ones for Disney's *That Darn Cat*, the horror movie *Squirm*, and the Charles Bronson pictures *The Evil That Men Do* and *Chato's Land*.

In the alley (near the Darwin Apartments, a nod to actor Darwin Joston from *Assault on Precinct 13*), Mickey is still trying to start his car. It's now dark and he's poking around under the hood with a flashlight. Suddenly, a big guy approaches him, intimidating him and revealing that he's the father of the little girl Mickey supposedly seduced. Realizing he's about to be assault, Mickey hops into the Mustang and turns the key again. This time it starts, and he burns rubber, speeding away into the night.

Back at Clarence's place, Clarence and Misty are in his bedroom. They are sitting on the floor beside the bed. Clarence is wearing a robe and Misty has tied his hands to a comic book stand. Misty wears only her blouse. They talk about Misty's newfound career as a call girl, and she informs him he's her first customer. (This is similar to Alabama's confession that Clarence is only her third customer in *True Romance*.) Misty reveals that she had previously been working in the music department at K-Mart. Clarence says he used to work at K-Mart, too, but worked in the shoe department. Typical of Tarantino's work, Clarence says he has a foot fetish, so he didn't mind.

Misty reveals that she chose to become a call girl after seeing Nancy Allen play one in *Dressed to Kill*. "She was cool, she was together," she says. "I looked at that film and looked at her part and I said to myself, 'Louise, that's the job for you.'" ("Misty" reveals her real name here.) This of course leads to Clarence waxing poetic about his love for (Tarantino's favorite director) Brian De Palma, calling him a "mean motor scooter." (The phrase, which originated in the Rudy Ray Moore song "The Human Tornado" from *Dolemite*, will later rear its head again in *From Dusk Till Dawn*.)

Clarence jokingly expresses a desire to see a law enacted that would force Nancy Allen to have sex with him whenever he wants. (Because when you're getting to know a woman, she wants

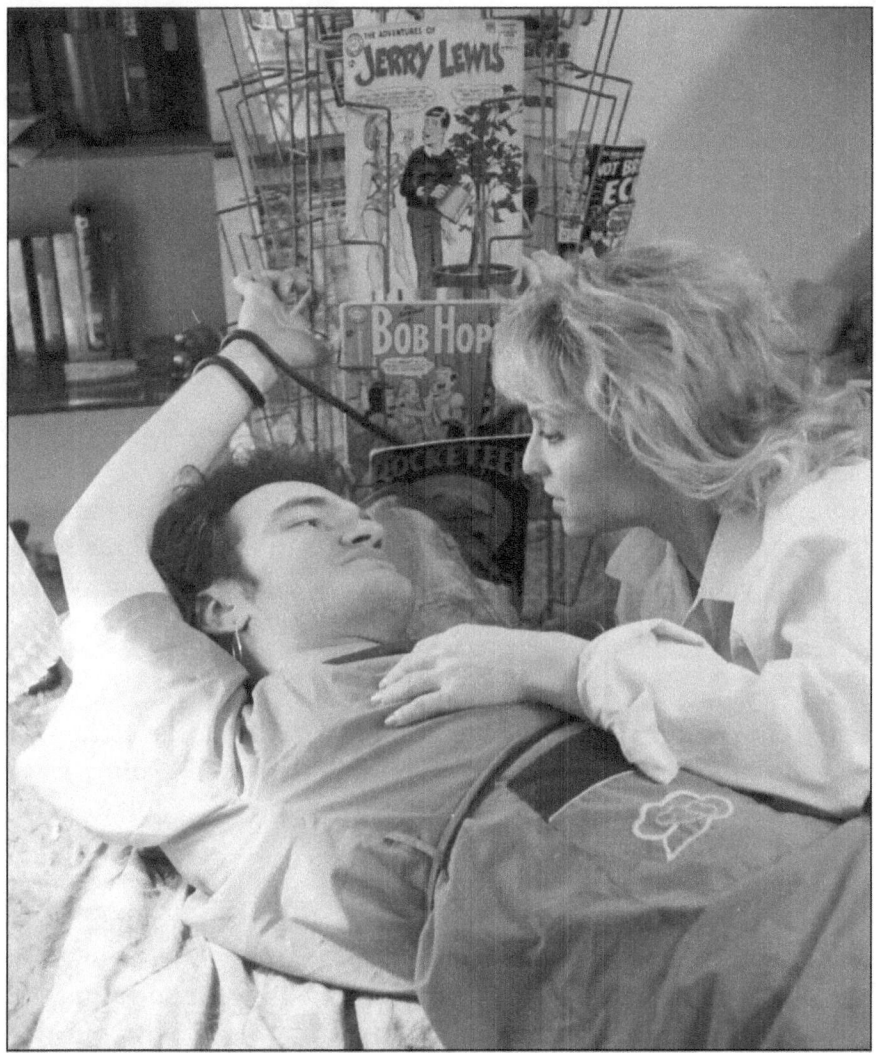

Misty (Crystal Shaw) has Clarence (Tarantino) bound to a comic book stand in this sexy scene. (Courtesy of Todd Henschell)

to hear about your desiring to bed other women, am I right?)

Misty and Clarence kiss. Misty asks him why he tried to set her up with Mickey instead of himself. He responds, "I don't know. I guess I'm just stupid." She then replies, "You're not stupid. Just wrong."

LINDA KAYE: There was one [time Tarantino quoted me in a script]... I commented to him that "this sounds familiar," and he said, "Well, it should. You said it."

The man's line was, "I guess I'm just stupid." I think prior to this the man had said something like, "I didn't think you liked me" or "I didn't know you cared" or something. Then he said, "I guess I'm just stupid." Then she said, "You're not stupid, you're just wrong." That's what I had said to him one day, and he ended up writing it into something. I said, "Did I say that?" He said yeah, and I said, "It sounds so much like a movie line now, but at the time it just seemed like the truth." And he said something to the effect of, "Well, maybe that's why it sounds so good as a movie line."

Back at the bar, Ronny is making himself a sandwich when Cecilia enters, dressed in her uniform. She asks where Clarence is, but Ronny plays dumb, believing Clarence is in trouble. This prompts Cecilia to produce her billy club and wave it in his face, threatening him. He ends up telling her that Clarence is at his apartment. When she leaves, he once again plays tough, muttering that she's lucky he didn't hurt her.

CRAIG HAMANN: Ronny takes a lot of abuse in the scene. It was the type of character Ronny could play so well. Ronny was really good casting for this. After we wrote the screenplay, we knew he would be perfect for the role.

An angry Mickey arrives at Clarence's apartment, wiping blood from his nose. He has a key to Clarence's apartment, so he unlocks the door and enters. When he finds no one in the front room, he checks in the bedroom, walking in on Clarence and Misty. In this scene there is another exchange of snappy rapid-fire *His Girl Friday*-type back-and-forth banter between the three characters as Mickey tries to understand what's happening.

CRAIG HAMANN: The dialogue in this scene is mine. This was intended as a tribute to Howard Hawks, who frequently used that type of dialogue. You've got a lot of someone saying something, someone questioning what they're saying, and then coming right back. Quentin and I were both big Howard Hawks fans.

Cecilia (Leeanne Chambers) intimidates Ronny the bartender (Ronald Coleman). (Courtesy of Todd Henschell)

Clarence and Mickey leave the room to talk. Clarence thinks Mickey's feelings are hurt, so he tries to console him. Mickey doesn't care about Clarence sleeping with Misty. He wants to tell Clarence about the crazy night he's had. Clarence says Misty has already told him about what happened and that he shouldn't feel bad. "It happens to everybody," he says. In their exchange it becomes apparent that Misty has lied to Clarence, telling him that she and Mickey tried to have sex, but Mickey was unable to achieve erection.

Clarence finally notices that Mickey's nose is bloody and asks him if he got in a fight. Clarence attempts to cheer him up and get him to eat some of the food he bought, but Mickey's not in the mood. Clarence continues trying to cheer him up. At one point he says, "Can you think of anyone, anyone at all, cooler than me?" Mickey considers the question and then answers Billy Joe Ewald, an employee at Video Archives. (Tarantino managed to pay homage to the store that served as his second home by squeezing in a reference here and by also showing it in the bakery scene.) Clarence says Billy Joe Ewald cannot be cooler than him because Billy Joe Ewald does not like Sonny Chiba films. After being reminded of this, Mickey says he cannot dispute this—Billy Joe Ewald is not cooler than Clarence.

Mickey then suggests another guy, Tommy Mero, who might be cooler than Clarence. Clarence shoots down this suggestion, too, reminding him that Tommy Mero doesn't like vanilla Cokes at Cafe Fifties. Once again Mickey has to agree, going so far as to call Mero an asshole. Clarence then says this fact made him write Mero out of his "cool book." Mickey then concedes that Clarence is the coolest cat he knows.

Clarence gives Mickey a birthday present. Clarence opens it and finds it's a video of *Rio Bravo*. (Yet another nod to Howard Hawks.) This is a tender moment where the two friends hug one another and feel close. Clarence then announces that they are still going to have a great party. He says Mickey can take a shower and relax first. Then afterwards, he says Misty can call a friend to come over and be Mickey's date. Mickey agrees.

CRAIG HAMANN: I wrote this scene. It was a really nice scene between Clarence and Mickey. Clarence is trying to talk Mickey up and make him feel better about his birthday, and Mickey's just kind of crying about everything. It was fun because we got to mention a few things we really liked here. One of those things was Sonny Chiba. Also, I made up the part about Clarence having a cool book. I said, "Clarence would have this book in which he writes about everything and everyone that's cool. He keeps track of all that." And Quentin loved that.

This scene really is Quentin and myself in real life. It was hyperbole, but in a lot of ways it defined our friendship. There was Quentin explaining his ideas about things, and then there was me being the straight man. It was a very intimate scene in a lot of ways, and it was a scene that we both really enjoyed doing. People don't know this, but it was very authentic and very autobiographical. It has always meant a lot to me, really. And you know what? The part where Clarence gives Mickey *Rio Bravo* for his birthday? That was real. Quentin really gave me *Rio Bravo* for my birthday.

It's weird, but for some reason this scene doesn't appear in all the videos circulating of *My Best Friend's Birthday*. There are different versions of the video out there.

The film then takes us back to the alley where Clifford is stuck upside down in a garbage can. A janitor named Klondike (Rick Squeri), carrying a bag of trash and a broom, finds him stuck there. He tries to free Clifford, but causes him to hit his head before eventually just dumping him out on the ground. Klondike then dusts the pimp off with his broom.

CRAIG HAMANN: This was a scene I wrote for Al and Rick. They were very good friends, so it was really nice to have them working together. We changed the scene a little bit when we were shooting, mainly due to the locations. But it didn't change too dramatically. It's still fairly close to what we had in the script. One of the things Quentin added when we were shooting was the opening of the scene. He had Klondike finding a life-sized cardboard Elvis Presley, which was actually owned by Quentin. Klondike says, "Wow, you never know what you're gonna find out here. This is cool!" I don't know if that footage still exists, but we did shoot it. The whole scene was a lot of fun and worked out really well.

Back at Clarence's apartment, Cecilia arrives to tell Clarence she's going to dump Eddie so they can be together. Cecilia owns a key and enters the apartment just as Mickey did before her. When she doesn't see anyone, she looks around. When she hears the shower running inside the bathroom, she enters, assuming it's Clarence. But it's not. It's Mickey. Cecilia pulls the shower door open and hilarity ensues, with neither of them knowing who the hell the other person is. After Cecilia asks Mickey if he and Clarence are gay lovers, Mickey tells her no and shuts the door.

CRAIG HAMANN: We shot this scene, and it was pretty funny. It ended up great. Leeane's delivery of, "You and Clarence don't go to gay bars together, do you?" was terrific. This whole scene was really funny. We shot it at Quentin's mother Connie's house. Everything in the movie that's supposed to be Clarence's apartment was shot there.

Cecilia goes to Clarence's bedroom, finding a blanket stretched over two chairs, like a child's makeshift pup tent. She hears Clarence and Misty giggling inside. Having heard the door open, Clarence mistakenly believes Cecilia is Mickey and says, "I love you, but you're gonna have to wait until I'm done here, and I'll find someone for you." Cecilia sees their silhouettes kissing and becomes upset, leaving the room.

Meanwhile, Clarence and Misty are looking at a book inside the tent.

> CLARENCE: There's nothing here on fellatio, but the *Guinness Book of World Records* record for kissing is three hours, twenty minutes.
>
> MISTY: Okay, we can do that.
>
> CLARENCE: Let's start now.

CRAIG HAMANN: The stuff about the *Guinness Book of World Records'* record for kissing was Quentin's. He came up with that.

CRYSTAL SHAW: When I look at the scenes where Quentin and I are talking and snuggling, kissing and discussing things...he's so good in that. If you look at his face, he's so loving. So romantic. The way he touched my chin, the way he said his dialogue. He's so romantic in that. I would love to see an amazing director tap into that part of him—the part most people don't see or probably know about.

Cecilia returns to the living room and starts drinking vodka punch. Mickey walks in a few moments later, now fully dressed. Mickey apologizes for yelling at Cecilia in the shower and says he thought her police uniform might have been a costume and that she was a call girl friend of Misty's. Cecilia, now becoming drunk, comes on to Mickey, aggressively attacking him with kisses.

The story returns to Clifford, walking down the street angrily, spouting humorously venomous lines.

CRAIG HAMANN: We never got to shoot this scene, although we were really looking forward to it. Al talking about being a "fiery furnace of hatred" and a "howling storm of revenge" would

Tarantino goes over Crystal Shaw's lines with her before shooting a scene. (Courtesy of Todd Henschell)

have been hilarious with his dry delivery. That would have been really good.

Now it's Eddie's turn to go to Ronny's bar and angrily ask where he can find Clarence, whom he refers to as the "rockabilly asshole." Ronny gives up the goods immediately this time, telling him where he can find Clarence. The address he provides is East Wood Apartments on Callahan Drive, apartment forty-four. (This is a reference to Clint Eastwood's *Dirty Harry* character, who carries a .44 Magnum.) Just as the running joke of characters showing up demanding Ronny tell them where Clarence is has been repeated, so is Ronny's after-the-fact tough guy routine. This time he remains quiet until after Eddie leaves and then says, "And stay out."

CRAIG HAMANN: Despite being the jerk he was, Dave was extremely good here, and it was one of his best scenes. Ronny was great, too. It was a really fun scene.

**Cecilia (Leeane Chambers) and Mickey (Craig Hamann) talk things out.
(Courtesy of Todd Henschell)**

Now it's Mickey and Cecilia's turn to make out in a blanket pup tent in the living room. As this is happening, Clarence and Misty walk towards the living room. Clarence is wearing a robe and Misty is wearing only her long blouse.

CLARENCE: I feel like Fred when he met Ginger.

MISTY: Really?

CLARENCE: Misty, I never lie about Fred and Ginger.

Misty is moved by this and she kisses Clarence. Clarence then announces that it's time to party. He yells, "Mickey, I have a poem!" He starts reading the poem he wrote for Mickey titled "Friendship." He's strolling through the apartment as he reads. As he and Misty approach, Mickey and Cecilia are caught off guard and hurriedly begin to dress. Misty sees them, but Clarence doesn't as he continues reading. Finally, Clarence sees Mickey and Cecilia half-dressed. Clarence becomes angry because Mickey has been making out with the woman he considers his girlfriend, but Mickey still doesn't know who she is or why he's upset. Cecilia then marches over to the table holding the food and snatches a can of whipped cream, turning and spraying it in Clarence's face. Misty sees this and becomes angry, and the two women start to fight.

Mickey tries to intervene, but Misty kicks him in the shin. Cecilia then grabs a cream pie and smashes it into his face. He stumbles and falls. Clarence then approaches the girls, trying to separate them, leading them both to shove him. Clarence stumbles, falling on top of Mickey, who then falls face first into the birthday cake. Misty and Cecilia continue to fight, falling down on the floor and rolling around.

Clarence and Mickey both stand. Mickey is completely covered with pie and cake. Clarence asks if he's angry, to which Mickey responds by spraying whipped cream in his face, stepping over the wrestling women, and leaving the room. Misty and Cecilia are oblivious to all this, and they continue fighting.

Outside the building, Eddie asks one of Clarence's neighbors (a character named Gilbert, who was never cast) where the apartment is. Gilbert says he doesn't know anyone named Clarence Poole. Eddie then asks if he knows where a "rockabilly asshole" lives, and Gilbert immediately knows who he's referring to. There's a funny exchange here where Eddie demands that Gilbert leave. Gilbert tells him he lives in the building, to which Eddie moves towards him menacingly, causing him to say he'll move. Eddie tells him to get his name changed while he's at it.

The story returns us to Ronny's bar. This time Clifford walks in. Ronny takes one look at him and blurts out Clarence's address.

Eddie shows up at Clarence's apartment, banging on the door and yelling. Cecilia and Misty are the only ones in the living room. Cecilia tells Misty that Eddie will kill them all if he gets inside. She says Eddie enjoys hurting people and has a difficulty stopping once he starts.

Inside the bathroom, Clarence is washing his face in the sink and talking to Mickey, who is inside the shower. Clarence is trying to smooth things over and is afraid Mickey will get depressed because of the nightmare his birthday has become. Mickey is still angry and doesn't want to talk. Clarence continues to apologize and then asks, "What else could possibly go wrong?"

On cue, Misty and Cecilia barge into the bathroom and inform Clarence and Mickey that Eddie will kill them. To this, Clarence acts tough, saying, "*When I get pissed, watch out!*"

In the living room, Eddie smashes in the front door with his .357 Magnum drawn. He's threatens to shoot Clarence when he finds him.

Everyone in the bathroom hears the threat. Cecilia suggests that maybe they should hide. Since this is a screwball comedy, this of course means that Clarence, Misty, and Cecilia all climb inside the shower with Mickey. Clarence advises Mickey to turn off the water so Eddie won't hear it.

> EDDIE: I'm gonna fire a warning shot, dickface, and then you better come out!

Eddie pulls the trigger, but realizes the gun isn't loaded. He then reaches for a quick load from his belt, but decides shooting Clarence will be too quick and too easy. He sits the gun on the table, deciding to fight Clarence hand-to-hand. Eddie begins tearing the apartment apart, searching for Clarence and Cecilia. In doing so, he spots some of Cecilia's clothes lying on the floor. He examines the blouse and then explodes into an angry fit.

Everyone else is still huddled together in the shower. Eddie makes his way through the apartment, kicking in doors. He expresses that he's anxious to hurt someone, concluding that Clarence must be in the bathroom because "where else would shit hide?"

Eddie bursts into the bathroom, finding everyone inside the shower together. "This is the sickest thing I've ever seen," he says. Eddie steps towards the shower, reaching back to punch. When he swings, everyone else ducks and he punches Mickey in the face. Mickey falls and everyone else tumbles out of the shower, falling onto Eddie.

As Mickey finally crawls out of the shower, praying for the nightmare to end, we see everyone else—Clarence, Eddie, Misty, and Cecilia—fighting. Eddie throws both women around and puts Clarence in a headlock. Mickey comes to the rescue and ends up in a fight with Eddie. They take turns punching and pushing each other and end up rolling around on the floor wrestling. Clarence charges towards Eddie. He goes to punch Eddie and Eddie ducks, causing Clarence to punch Mickey in the face again, knocking him unconscious. Clarence being Clarence, he tells Eddie he should look at what he's just done to Mickey, warning him that he will do the same to him.

Eddie punches Clarence in the mouth, knocking him out. Eddie continues acting macho, asking the girls if they want punched also.

Suddenly, Clifford barges into the apartment, inadvertently slamming the door against Eddie, who then bounces into the wall. Now Eddie is unconscious, as are Clarence and Mickey.

CRAIG HAMANN: Quentin let me do the choreography for this scene. I had to explain to everyone what I wanted them to do physically. They all worked really hard and tried their best. We got into this whole thing where there's some wrestling and people are screaming at each other. Quentin kept referring to it as a brouhaha, and that's basically what it was—one big brouhaha with lots of people doing lots of different things; everybody being crazy, their personalities, the weirdness, all coming to a head right here.

Clifford demands that Misty leave with him, but she refuses. He tries to grab her, but she knees him in the groin and he falls to his knees. Cecilia then stuffs a wastebasket over his head and he falls to the floor.

The two women are now staring at a room filled with unconscious men. Cecilia and Misty both express that they're sick of men. Cecilia tells Misty she could arrest her for being a prostitute, but says she won't. She then tells her she could become a police officer "like Nancy Allen in *RoboCop*."

The women take turns telling their goodbyes to each of the four now semi-conscious men on the floor, ranging from Cecilia telling Mickey "you're kind of nice, but never again... I don't like your friends," to Misty calling Clifford a "lousy pimp." They then leave to get a drink (but not at Ronny's Bar, which they mock before leaving).

Once the women are gone, the four guys struggle to stand. There's another humorous conversation here where no one really knows what's happening. The men all lament about the women they've lost.

> EDDIE: Do you know what it's like to have the woman you love watch you with admiration while you smash some faggot's head in with your nightstick?

> CLIFFORD: No.

> EDDIE: It's ecstasy...and now it's gone.

Mickey becomes angry and yells that he doesn't understand what's going on, and then warns everyone that he'll kill the next person who talks about anything he doesn't understand. Clarence says that Mickey has a point and that complaining isn't helping their situation.

> CLARENCE: I suggest we stop dickin' around, count our losses, lick our wounds, and go to Ronny's Bar. Maybe after a few beers we can make sense outta all this.

The four men go to the bar and have a round of beers. After the first beer, Eddie leaves, saying he's going to go bust some heads to help mend his broken heart. Mickey and Clarence start to recount the fight. When they discuss Clarence accidentally punching Mickey in the face and knocking him out, Clarence starts to brag about how hard a hitter he is.

The clock strikes midnight and it's now officially Mickey's birthday. Clarence still wants to party, but Mickey takes him outside to talk to him. They end up sitting on the hood of a parked car. Mickey says he's depressed and doesn't want to party. But Clarence gets him engaged in conversation and they start talking about how they're similar to Crockett and Tubbs from *Miami Vice*, causing them both to become excited. Mickey begins to cheer up, and Clarence eventually convinces him to do his impersonation of Dirty Harry. Now they are both having a good time, and Mickey is no longer sad.

CRAIG HAMANN: This was a nice scene between Mickey and Clarence, where they're just talking and we can get a better look at the dynamics of their relationship. Once again, Clarence is coming to the rescue as far as building Mickey up. He's makes him feel better and he's trying to calm him down. This scene was actually shot outside an apartment complex, but we were still able to make it look like the exterior of the bar.

Clarence produces a joint and hands it to Mickey, telling him to smoke it, get relaxed, and then come back inside to party. Mickey agrees. Clarence tells Mickey happy birthday. The two friends hug and Mickey tells Clarence he's his best friend. Clarence goes inside.

Now alone, Mickey lights the joint and takes a drag. Suddenly, red and blue lights begin flashing. Mickey turns and looks back, seeing that all this time they've been sitting on the hood of a police cruiser. A cop gets out and walks up to Mickey, shining a flashlight in his face as Mickey sits there with a joint in his hand.

CRAIG HAMANN: We weren't able to do as good a job as we would have liked with the police car, but we got it done. We had a friend of Quentin's who was working security at this apartment complex, and he had a security car with flashers on it. In the dark, it looks like a police car. And when he gets out of the car with the security guard uniform on, he's got the gun, the cap, and the badge, so he looks like a cop.

The one thing that we would have liked to have shot over again was the revelation at the very end. It was difficult to obscure the fact that Mickey's on a police car before he realizes it. It was tough, even though we only had the front of the car sticking out from an alley. We shot at one angle and you saw them sitting on the hood, and then when you swung around, you could see it was a police car. Of course, we had the lights flashing before that. But it was hard to do that because we didn't have the right lights and equipment to do it right. And that was always a bit of a problem—having the right equipment. We had to work with what we had. Sometimes we could rent something decent, but we could only afford to rent it for a while. We didn't have money to keep things as long as we needed them. Sometimes we had to use our brains and get really, really experimental. But that was the film school dynamic of making the movie. We would make mistakes or need things we didn't have, and we would learn how to work around them.

And Quentin is like that. The thing that's beautiful about him as a director is that he's the type of person who doesn't even have the word "can't" in his vocabulary. He finds a way to work around a problem or work through it. He was always coming up with something. That was a large part of making this film, and that was a dynamic that was extremely beneficial to *My Best Friend's Birthday*. It was beneficial for everyone.

Quentin and I both loved making the film. I have enjoyed going back over the experience now that we're talking about it, but I wouldn't want to repeat it. I never want to be that ill-prepared for anything ever again. I want to make a movie, and I want to direct again, but if it does happen, I want to be a stickler for preparation. I want to have the right camera, the right lens, the right lights, the right dolly.

Most low-budget movies don't have a very good script. I think what Quentin and I wrote, for what we were trying to do, was pretty good. I'm not patting us on the back, but I think it worked. And as far as the direction, I thought Quentin, for a first-time director, was terrific. His talent was already starting to emerge, and you could see that right there on the set. That was what made *My Best Friend's Birthday* different from other low-budget films—we had Quentin. It's hard to go wrong when you have that kind of untapped genius there.

I know some people have watched the footage of the film that's leaked online and they say this is a piece of crap. Fine, they can say that. But you know what? It's a hell of a lot better than it would have been without Quentin there. He elevated everything in the film, and he did it in a masterfully.

www.ingramcontent.com/pod-product-compliance
Lightning Source LLC
Chambersburg PA
CBHW030109170426
43198CB00009B/557